Uttar Pradesh: The Road Ahead

Published in association with
Observer Research Foundation
New Delhi

Observer Research Foundation (ORF) is a public policy think-tank that aims to influence formulation of policies for building a strong and prosperous India. The ORF pursues these goals by providing informed and productive inputs, in-depth research and stimulating discussion. The Foundation is supported in its mission by a cross-section of India's leading public figures, academics and business leaders.

Uttar Pradesh

The Road Ahead

Edited by
Venkitesh Ramakrishnan

ACADEMIC FOUNDATION
NEW DELHI

ACADEMIC FOUNDATION

First published in 2009
by

ACADEMIC FOUNDATION
4772-73 / 23 Bharat Ram Road, (23 Ansari Road),
Darya Ganj, New Delhi - 110 002 (India).
Phones : 23245001 / 02 / 03 / 04.
Fax : +91-11-23245005.
E-mail : books@academicfoundation.com
www. academicfoundation.com

in association with the
Observer Research Foundation, New Delhi

Cataloging in Publication Data--DK
Courtesy: D.K. Agencies (P) Ltd. <docinfo@dkagencies.com>

Uttar Pradesh: the road ahead / edited by Venkitesh Ramakrishnan.
p. cm.
Contributed articles on socioeconomic policies of contemporary Uttar Pradesh, India.

ISBN 13: 9788171887835
ISBN 10: 817188783X

1. Uttar Pradesh (India)--Politics and government--21st century. 2. Uttar Pradesh (India)--Social policy. 3. Uttar Pradesh (India)--Economic policy. 4. Regional planning--India--Uttar Pradesh. I. Ramakrishnan, Venkitesh.

DDC 320.9542 22

Typeset by Italics India, New Delhi.
Printed and bound in India.

Contents

About the Editor/Contributors

Editor:

Venkitesh Ramakrishnan, Deputy Editor, Frontline magazine, The Hindu group of publications.

Contributors:

M.P. Dube, Director, Institute of Gandhian Thought and Peace Studies, University of Allahabad.

Gyanesh Kudaisya, Associate Professor, South Asian Studies Programme, National University, Singapore.

Santosh Mehrotra, Senior Adviser, Rural Development Division, Planning Commission, Government of India.

Salil Misra, Faculty of History, Indira Gandhi National Open University, New Delhi.

Yogendra Narain (IAS), Former Chief Secretary Uttar Pradesh and Former Secretary-General, Rajya Sabha.

Sudha Pai, Professor, Centre for Political Studies, Jawaharlal Nehru University, New Delhi and Senior Fellow, Nehru Memorial Museum and Library, New Delhi.

Anand Sarup, Former Secretary, Planning and Chairman, State Planning Institute, Uttar Pradesh.

V.J. Ravi Shankar, Lead Economist, South Asia Economic Management, The World Bank.

R.R. Shah (IAS), Former Member-Secretary, Planning Commission, Government of India.

Ajit Kumar Singh, Director, Giri Institute of Development Studies, Lucknow.

Jagpal Singh, Reader, Faculty of Political Science, School of Social Sciences, New Delhi.

Prakash Singh (IPS), Former Director-General Police, Uttar Pradesh and Former Director-General, Border Security Force.

Ravi Srivastava, Member, National Commission for Enterprises in the Unorganised Sector, Government of India.

S.C. Tripathi (IAS), Former Secretary, Ministry of Petroleum, Government of India, New Delhi.

Hariraj Singh Tyagi, Ex-MLC, Meerut, Uttar Pradesh.

Foreword

Uttar Pradesh is by far the largest state in the country. Because of the size of the State, developments in it make a significant impact on national polity. It is also one of the most backward states in the country. In terms of economic and human development, it presents a depressing picture. The per capita income of Uttar Pradesh, which was on par with the national level at the time of Independence, is now roughly half of the national level. The economic growth of the state has been slow and halting, leading to very high incidence of poverty. It has stayed well below the national average in family planning and its high birth rate has created a great population pressure. Its economy is still largely agriculture-oriented and agricultural productivity is low. The state is also characterised by low social indicators. Levels of education are dismal and the incidence of illiteracy is high. The availability of public health services is very poor.

Uttar Pradesh is also marked by sharp inter-regional variations in terms of economic and social development. The western region is relatively more prosperous, the central and Bundelkhand regions fall in the middle and the eastern region is the poorest. Naxalite activity has begun to affect some parts of the state.

Uttar Pradesh has gone through a period of considerable political instability in the last two decades or so. This has taken its toll on the administrative systems of the state. Far from boasting about good governance which was the hallmark of Uttar Pradesh administration, the state is now among the most poorly administered states of the country.

Against this background, the Observer Research Foundation (ORF) commissioned a study last year to analyse the factors that have kept Uttar Pradesh from achieving its potential of social and economic growth, with a view to generating an informed dialogue on this subject. Based on this study, a seminar was held on 23rd and 24th May 2008 in New Delhi with the theme "Uttar Pradesh: The Road Ahead". The seminar was well attended by a large number of eminent participants from Government of India, Government of UP and the World Bank, and from the fields of politics, administration, academia and civil society. The deliberations covered a wide range of subjects relating to social and economic development and to governance of the state. Discussions also covered the issue of regional disparities and in this context, the pros and cons of the division of the state into smaller units were examined.

It is hoped that this report of the seminar would serve to highlight the problems being faced by Uttar Pradesh and would assist in formulation of policies that would lead to betterment of the lives of the citizens of this large state. ORF proposes to continue the process of engagement with Uttar Pradesh in order to present well-analysed policy options to policy makers to assist them in their task.

Surendra Singh
President,
ORF Centre for Politics and Governance

Introduction

The chapters in this volume address and evaluate four important aspects of contemporary Uttar Pradesh society. These are: a) the new trajectories in the political process and their impact and potential in the short, medium and long term; b) the economy and development—their present status and the way forward; c) the challenges to and prospects of good governance; and d) regional disparities and the case for smaller geographical and administrative units. Being the most populous State and the one that contributes the maximum number of members to the Parliament, any study on its political, economic and social life evokes interest, but the historical context in which the chapters in this volume have been presented give them an added significance. This context has been created by the new political trajectories that have opened up in the State during and after the 2007 Assembly elections, which witnessed the return of a single party government after a gap of over 15 years. In fact, issues related to political economy, governance and development have been addressed systematically through a number of studies over the past three decades or so, but these new political developments have opened up these studies to review and scrutiny for fresh nuances and dimensions in context of the changed scenario in the State. The chapters in this volume seek to encompass these nuances and dimensions and chart out a course for all the four areas that are addressed by this volume.

The book has been divided into following four thematic sections:

1. New Social Consensus in Uttar Pradesh: Problems and Possibilities
2. Development of Uttar Pradesh: Performance and Prospects
3. Governance and Administration of Uttar Pradesh
4. Regionalism in Uttar Pradesh: A Case for Reorganisation of State

Each section has a lead chapter which analyses the issues addressed by the chapter historically and, in a futuristic sense, charts out the possible direction to take in the days to come. The accompanying chapters supplement the lead chapter by highlighting a specific dimension of the issue or by espousing a distinctive perspective on it. The concluding chapter "An Overview and Some

Projections", sums up the four thematic segments and delineates an overall approach. Central to the discourse is the return of a politically stable single party government, the Mayawati-led Bahujan Samaj Party (BSP) Ministry, in May 2007. For nearly a decade and a half before that, instability had plagued UP in the form of identity politics. The obvious outcome was poor governance and administration, aggravating the economic backwardness of the State as also intensifying regional disparities. The chapters have integrated the cumulative experience of Uttar Pradesh in the 15 years between 1992 and 2007 and while doing so, brought up the opportunities provided to the State in political, social, economic and developmental terms by the 2007 May verdict. Collectively, the discourse advanced by the volume could well be perceived as a broad framework for evolving new strategies for inclusive growth of Uttar Pradesh and bring these strategies to fruition.

New Social Consensus in Uttar Pradesh: Problems and Possibilities

What exactly are the social and political dimensions of the 2007 verdict? What would be its impact on and influence over society and polity in the short, medium and long term? These are the principal questions addressed by the first part of the book.

The BSP's momentous triumph in the 2007 polls was mainly on account of two factors. The first factor, the anti-incumbency sentiment, is a universal disadvantage that can confront any ruling party. In this case, it was manifested in the consolidation of a large majority of the anti-incumbency vote against the Mulayam Singh Yadav-led Samajwadi Party (SP) Government that was in power for approximately three years. The second factor was, in many ways, unique to the State and had manifested itself as a new, path-breaking dimension to/in identity politics, in vogue since the late 1980s. It was the BSP ideated socio-political plank of Dalit-Brahmin *Bhaichara* (brotherhood). The party had built up this plank painstakingly over a period of two and half years (following the Lok Sabha elections of April-May 2004), paying attention to minute political and organisational factors at the grassroots. The novel coalition proved to be a powerful magnet in the political arena, attracting to the BSP, large segments of anti-incumbency vote from the minority Muslim community, various Other Backward Castes (OBC) and Most Backward Castes (MBCs), severely undermining the electoral bases of the two national parties, the Indian National Congress and the Bharatiya Janata Party (BJP).

The primary question that the first part of the volume addresses is whether this new social coalition is stable enough to significantly and durably impact and influence the political process in UP. All the four chapters in this section address this question from varied perspectives and with distinctive emphasis. Obviously, the segment offers no panache, but underlines the possibilities that have opened up, as well as some of the challenges it faces in the altogether new situation.

The lead chapter in this section, by Sudha Pai, perceives the ascent of the BSP and its leader Mayawati to single party chief ministership as a development with implications not only for the state but also for national politics. According to her, the aggregation of seemingly disparate socio-political support bases (Dalits and Brahmins) that the BSP successfully put together is the most concrete manifestation of the effort of parties pursuing 'politics of identity' to construct broad, aggregative, social rainbow identities and build new alignments based on them. Dr. Pai points out that, since its formation in 1984, the BSP has constantly reinvented its identity and changed its strategies of electoral mobilisation *vis-à-vis* other political parties. It has moved from an almost puritanical and hostile approach, characteristic of a narrow identity based movement-cum-party to a more moderate and electorally oriented political party in response to the changing political situation, at the same time remaining within the larger framework defined by the Dalit identity and the ideology of Ambedkarism. Dr. Pai further holds that, if the BSP is able to take its success in forging the social alliance from the arena of elections to that of governance, it could virtually lead to a kind of paradigm shift not only in UP politics but also in national politics. This paradigm shift, the chapter ventures to say, could even result in the development of a pan-Indian identity for the BSP, which in turn would ensure a greater role for the party in national politics. Even while stating this, the chapter stresses on the challenges that the new dispensation faces, in terms of its political initiatives as well as governance strategies. The chapter points out that one of the major challenges would be in maintaining a balance between the interests of Dalits and upper castes, while seeking to implement a broad based and inclusive agenda of development. The same qualitative challenge of maintaining the Dalit-Brahmin *Bhaichara* would be reflected in political and social terms too at the grassroot level. The challenge can be addressed only by effecting a proper balance in meeting the political and economic expectations of the upper caste on the one side and on the other, its core group, the Dalits and other social groups that have voted it to power. Dr. Pai's chapter stresses that it is imperative for the BSP to lay emphasis on economy and governance. For, these would be the two principal instruments through which the government and the entire political dispensation could advance the new social consensus and create a long-term impact, in the state and the nation.

In the second chapter, Hariraj Singh Tyagi argues that the BSP's 2007 election strategy was essentially opportunistic and, though it has paid dividends in electoral terms, it has blunted the sharpness of the revolutionary movement of Dalits and other lower castes. "Kanshi Ram and hundreds of his comrades had worked hard to give this movement a steady momentum and taking it to newer and newer heights. Mayawati came to this movement during its last glorious phase. She is not its creator or inspirer. Therefore, in this majority rule of hers, all programmes of Dalit upliftment and consciousness have slowed down and at places have even become defunct. Not only this, in her reign, incidents of atrocities against Dalits and their oppression has gone up." Tyagi points out that government statistics itself has revealed the rise in incidents of Dalit oppression under the new regime. He also argues that the contention of the government about the improved registration of cases as a reason for this rise is not valid.

With the clarion call of "Bahujan Hitay Bahujan Sukhay", Dr. Ambedkar and Kanshi Ram generated a revolution that aimed at demolishing the caste-class ridden system. Mayawati replaced this call with that of "Sarvajan Hitay, Sarvajan Sukhay". This is a deceptive and dishonest slogan and by using it she might have secured a majority in connivance with the upper caste, but who can ignore the ugly reality that these very castes and classes look down upon Dalits and backwards with utter contempt. In politics, one fundamental principle must be kept in mind and it is that a party which deviates from its fundamental values, original ideology, original principles and programmes and resorts to opportunistic path to power, in course of time, becomes irrelevant and gets marginalised. In Tyagi's view, the Congress and BJP in Uttar Pradesh are clear examples of this political burn-out.

The third chapter by Salil Mishra advances the discourse further and points out that, historically, there have been many instances in UP of political experiments that brought together socially disparate groups, but most of them have not been able to take their own self-professed agenda forward in a concrete and comprehensive manner. Salil Mishra specifically points out that what happened in the last elections should best be understood as an episode. "Episodes do not necessarily constitute trends, they can also be aberrations."

Citing from various political developments since the 1940s, Mishra pointed out that UP's politics is a story of multiple factions and various identities associated with them floating in and out of different political and ideological formulations. No dilution or diffusion of identities has occurred in this process. There has been no fixity of identities and yet no dilution either. This, Mishra points out, has been the paradox of UP's political life. The chapter argues that any meaningful social consensus would require, among others, the following pre-conditions: (a) marriage between political alliance and social alliance; (b) process of mobility not just across factions and identities, but within the political formation itself; and (c) enough tenacity and resilience in political contracts to undermine status. This change from status to contract in the larger sociological sense was one of the factors identified by Mishra. The chapter argues that while there is an emergence of a contract between the various social communities and partners in the consensus, there has been no basic change in terms of status.

The fourth chapter in this section by Venkitesh Ramakrishnan makes the point that the BSP, in the new context, would have to make a course-correction *vis-à-vis* its political and organisational strategies it has followed so far. The BSP's history of the past two decades has been one of assertive Dalit politics that by-passed well-defined ideological positions or engagement in concrete ideological debates. Right from the times of the BSP founder Kanshi Ram, the argument has been that the most important thing for the party was for the "Bahujan Samaj" (read Dalit society) to capture power and, once that was done, all other ideological, political, social requisites for a just society would follow. Venkitesh Ramakrishnan's chapter argues that the new political context created by the party would impel it to go beyond such simplistic political projections and work towards an ideologically well-defined political action plan.

Development of Uttar Pradesh: Performance and Prospects

The economic situation of Uttar Pradesh over the last two decades has been a point of debate in a number of studies. The unanimous verdict of all these studies has been that the state is consistently and systematically moving on a downhill course. With this background, the chapters in this section raise three important questions. One: Would the new social and political scenario post-May 2007 elections result in a course correction that would impact the economic growth of Uttar Pradesh in a significantly positive manner? Two:

Qualitatively, what are the areas of the economy where improvements and course correction are possible? Three: What would be the mechanism for implementing this course correction?

There are four chapters in this segment too, with the lead chapter by Ajit Kumar Singh. The chapter provides a broad analysis of the economic situation of the state with the premise that "all the indicators of economic and social development for UP present a rather dismal and depressing picture: low per capita income, slow economic growth, high birth rates, widespread poverty, high IMR and MMR, low literacy especially among females, poor health outcomes, high incidence of child and women nutritional deficiency. In all these indicators, UP ranks among the bottom 3-4 states among the major states of India. It invariably ranks at 14th or 15th position in terms of economic and social indicators as numerous studies have shown." The three other chapters focus on specific areas of the economy. Santosh Mehrotra's chapter makes a comprehensive analysis of the health sector in Uttar Pradesh while Ravi Srivastava examines the employment situation and delineates the direction required to bring about positive changes in this area of the economy. V. Ravi Shankar's chapter focuses on some of the structural adjustments made in recent years and the salutary effect they have had on the economic system as a whole and proposes how they can be taken forward.

The lead chapter goes beyond the well-known and dismal statistics on economic parameters of the state and identifies some of its qualitative deficiencies too. These are classified under the following heads: Poor Infrastructure; Distortionay Policy and Regulatory Regime; Governance Issues; and Absence of Development-oriented Leadership. The chapter highlights the fundamental problems of infrastructure and delivery. To give an example, the power situation in Uttar Pradesh is so poor that the talk about further industrialisation falls flat when the supply is not sufficient even to run the existing industries. The same goes for roads. There is no basic infrastructure of roads for the people and goods, not to speak of industrial development. The chapter tells us there is a spate of excellent policy and research documents from government and other sources gathering dust, never to see the light of day. Also highlighted are the lack of stable policies, as also honest governance and administration by various past governments, as well as the blighted law and order situation in the state. On policy and programme thrusts needed to effect a turnaround in the economy, the chapter says: "To push up the rate of growth of the state economy, investment levels have to be substantially augmented. While the need of public investment in required economic and social infrastructure is clearly there, bulk of investment has to come through the private sector. Hence, the first priority of the state should be to create a suitable investment climate and the bottlenecks faced by the industry have to be removed. Removing the infrastructure gap deserves the highest priority. The most critical requirement at present is the improvement in power situation, without which one cannot expect high industrial and agricultural growth. Improvement in road network and better connectivity to villages are needed to unleash the growth potential of the state, particularly in the rural areas. The initiatives that the present state government has taken to promote investment in infrastructure through public-private participation are a welcome step.

Equally important is to step up an attractive and conducive policy environment to attract investment to the state. The distorted economic policies affecting the working of the land, labour and product market have to be set right to make UP industrially competitive. The process of economic reforms and deregulation has to be speeded up. Procedures have to be streamlined and simplified and regulatory burden eased. System of automatic and time bound clearance through web-enabled systems has to be put in place as some other states have done. Discretionary controls have to be minimised to reduce opportunities for rent seeking.

Wide ranging governance reforms have to be undertaken with a view to improve the law and order situation, minimise corruption, improve the functioning of government organisations. Transparency, accountability and responsiveness of administration are the hallmark of good governance. The management of critical infrastructure like power, roads and irrigation has to be professionalised."

V. Ravi Shankar's chapter notes that there have been improvements in many UP sectors in the last few years. Agriculture has performed relatively well, tough industries lag behind rest of India. These gains are dogged by poor infrastructure and red tape. These problems have become a constraint on the private sector too, especially on small and medium enterprises. Fiscal reform has expanded the budget space, but translating outlays to outcome is a big challenge. Lack of accountability has resulted in low quality services and programmes for the poor, says Dr. Shankar, adding that politics of dignity and development being advanced by the Bahujan Samaj Party would ensure a greater commitment to improve law and order, increase employment and welfare for all. This is because the core political constituency of the BSP consists of people who have been oppressed for several decades—nay, for centuries. He foresees that the overall positive developments in fiscal areas would lead to better delivery of social and economic services to the people, especially because the aggregate fiscal situation has improved since 2000.

Ravi Srivastava's chapter on employment in UP analyses the scenario and discusses the strategies required to improve the sector. Srivastava says that though the State has lower unemployment levels than states like Kerala, the bulk of the employment in UP falls in the low productive sectors. UP has a higher proportion of informal employment (92.5 per cent) as compared to the national average (86.3 per cent) and 59.8 per cent of the state's workforce is still in the agriculture sector. Hence, the principal focus of any future planning has to focus on the quality of employment so as to raise it from the low productive sectors. Emphasis has to be laid on the higher productive sectors and at the same time, a fillip has to be given to low productive sectors in order to increase productivity. Srivastava suggests a greater focus on sunrise sectors, such as cultural tourism.

Santosh Mehrotra's chapter studies the ailing health sector and prescribes the measures for cure. Pointing out that 58 per cent of poverty in India is geographically concentrated in the so-called 'BIMARU' states, it says that UP covers a major area of this health deficiency region. Yet, strangely enough, the state's health data do not sound that bad. According to government statistics, as compared to the national average of 1.45 lakh population served per government hospital, the figure for UP is 1.98 lakh. The figure for Bihar is 8.7 lakh. Whatever be the statistics, the ground reality is far from satisfactory. The state government's health expenditure per capita, at Rs.84, is far below the national average of Rs. 207. Doctors and the medical staff are bereft of any commitment, sense of duty or even human compassion and nothing has been done to change this attitude or situation. Dr. Mehrotra suggests the authorities should concentrate on primary and promotive public interventions as well as population-based health interventions. The chapter perceives the National Rural Health Mission (NRHM) as a vehicle to enforce a number of remedial steps.

Governance and Administration of Uttar Pradesh

The third section of this volume focuses on issues of governance and administration in UP. The lead chapter by Yogendra Narain, the former Chief Secretary of the state, provides a panoramic perspective on the problems that confront the systems of governance. The other chapters in this section are by Anand Sarup, the former Union Education Secretary, Rajeev Ratna Shah, the former member Secretary of the National Planning Commission and Prakash Singh, the former Director General of Police. The lead chapter maintains that the bane of the state was the lack of delivery and corruption at various levels of governance. "Governance in Uttar Pradesh has been marked by political instability and even a deeper instability in the bureaucracy," he says and goes on to add: "Since Independence UP has had 42 chief secretaries, out of whom only 3 stayed on for more than 3 years, while just 5 stayed on for more than 2 years and 38 chief ministers in addition to 3 spells of President's rule. With growing political instability leading to coalition governments the Chief Minister, of whichever party, has to make various compromises both on policy issues as well as administrative issues. This has led to a tendency to maximise short-term gains rather than addressing the long-term issues concerning the economic development of the state. This has led to short tenure of the district officers and secretaries in the government of Uttar Pradesh and has also encouraged amongst officers, the tendency to be closer to the powers than being independent in taking decisions. This has played havoc with all public organisations in the state." The chapter argues that, on the whole, an assessment of the systems of governance and administration in the last 15 years would hold them as a failure, both in terms of outcome as well as in terms of public perception. While there is no official data on the degree of corruption in the state, a survey conducted in 2000 at the instance of the World Bank highlighted the all-pervasive corruption in the lower judiciary, the revenue department, sales tax department and the local bodies. In successive surveys of the business community by the journal *Business Today*, the perception of administrative corruption and malfeasance was cited as a major deterrent against investment in the state. The lead chapter contends that three firm measures are an imperative for improving the quality of governance. First, a redefinition of the role of government, specifically a reduction of its role in the economy through deregulation and disinvestments, so that it is able to focus its limited capacity in those areas in which it has comparative advantages. Second, a programme of civil service renewal is required so that the government can better perform its core functions. Third, significant gains in service quality and accountability by well planned devolution of spending responsibilities and revenue raising powers to elected local bodies. In the areas of civil service reform too, the government faces three critical challenges. It must enhance the productivity of the civil services and ensure that every employee is performing socially relevant tasks. Secondly, it must create procedures for awarding merit and for punishing malfeasance and misconduct so as to enforce accountability and performance. Thirdly, the cutting edge level of the civil services has to be adequately trained and professionalised.

The piece by Prakash Singh, a former DGP of the State, highlights the collapse of the administrative structure and the law and order machinery in Uttar Pradesh. The piece argues that several factors ranging from political interference to casteism to nepotism have contributed to this degeneration, but the central factor is the rampant corruption in the administrative and law and order machinery. Prakash Singh's account draws majorly on his personal experience as a senior police officer of long standing in Uttar Pradesh.

The chapter by Anand Sarup focuses on structural devices, such as formation of non-partisan committees to advance the developmental process in an unprejudiced manner. Sarup opts for a mechanism to study regional issues too in detail and address questions of governance and administration from that perspective. R.R. Shah's chapter throws light on how e-Governance practices could help lessen corruption in the bureaucracy and provide better delivery systems to the people. The chapter provides both a macro-picture of e-Governance initiatives and a micro-picture, looking at different departments and possible interventions.

Regionalism in Uttar Pradesh: A Case for Reorganisation of State

The last thematic section advances the discussion on economy and governance to raise the question: Can the problem of increasing regional disparities be solved by a reorganisation of the state? The points raised in the chapters of this section are important because of the demands that have been made from time to time for the division of the state into smaller units. The demands for units such as Bundelkhand, Poorvanchal and Harit Pradesh have specifically come up. The lead chapter is by Gyanesh Kudaisya. Normally, any discussion of geographical division of a state evaluates the administration, economic aspects, cultural aspects and political aspects. However, Kudaisya veers from this conventional method and takes a larger, historical perspective. The chapter points out that the different regions of the state were brought together into one administrative unit by an external action during the pre-Independence period. Hence the question: Is the identity of UP as one single unit solid enough to keep it going forward and developing as a single unit? Admitting that it may not be necessary to carve out different geographical or administrative units from the current entity, the chapter, however, insists that this question should be addressed in all its dimensions and adds that such an application could well lead to new kinds of states, which have alternate parameters of governance. This new type of states could well move away from the heartland administration and its ideological legacies and focus on concepts such as representative and inclusive administrations and decentralisation. In short, Kudaisya's historical view points towards a conceptual re-division of the heartland identity of UP rather than a physical re-division.

Other chapters in the section, such as those by Jagpal Singh and M.P. Dube highlight the growth of regional imbalances caused by the existence of a monolithic state and make a case for its re-division. However, clear geographical parameters of the proposed states are not given in the chapters. The fourth chapter in this section by S.C. Tripathi brings in the expertise of a bureaucrat to the debate and points out that while a consideration of regional imbalances and solutions to it could well lead to the demands for geographical and administrative reorganisation, it is also required to deliberate on the costs involved to carry out an exercise of this dimension. What needs to be analysed is not just the financial costs and the administrative expenditure, but also other qualitative and subjective factors. The qualitative factors include the lack of strong political demand for the re-division and the absence of an emotional dimension to the demands that are being made, at least at this point of time.

Editor's Note:

An important coordinate of all the papers and presentations in this volume was the political situation prevailing in Uttar Pradesh in May 2008, when the ORF seminar on Uttar Pradesh took place. There have been a number of developments since then—including the 2009 April-May Lok Sabha elections—and these developments have altered some of the contexts and premises advanced in the papers and presentations in the volume. These changes, however, have in no way detracted the historical and thematic relevance of the volume and the perspectives put forth in it.

I

New Social Consensus in Uttar Pradesh: Problems and Possibilities

1 The New Politics of Mayawati

Implications for State and National Politics

Sudha Pai

The end of the single party rule at the Centre and in some states in the 1990s has given political developments in the states greater significance than in the national scene, more so to larger, highly populated states like Uttar Pradesh. The BSP's single-party victory in the 2007 State Assembly elections ushered in a new era, following as it did a decade of hung Assemblies. The two big national parties, the BJP and the Congress performed miserably, leaving the field open for the SP and the BSP. More importantly, the BSP won over 30 per cent of the votes and was able to form a single party government for the first time. It owed its victory to its new strategy of building an aggregative "social rainbow" identity by gaining the support of the upper castes and by promising a more inclusive developmental agenda. The BSP leadership is now keen to replicate the experiment of "social engineering" in other states and emerge as a key player at the Centre. It has been said and heard that Mayawati's eyes are on the premiership, as also that her organisation is already making preparations for the electoral campaign for the 2009 Lok Sabha elections. All that, however, are premature conjectures; what is of consequence today is that the BSP has emerged as an important actor on the national scene where both the Congress and the BJP are no more the strong, nationwide forces they were, and the Left being confined to only three states.

This chapter examines whether the BSP leadership, having achieved an absolute majority in the 2007 Assembly elections will be able to deal with the new challenges it now faces. These are: maintaining the upper-lower castes social alliance by implementing a broad-based and inclusive agenda of development and, moving beyond UP to develop a pan-Indian identity and play a central role in national politics. The chapter argues that these are formidable tasks and the achievement of the first will, to a large extent, determine the success of the second. The BSP will have to balance the political and economic expectations of the state's upper castes and other social groups that have helped vote it to power, as well as the demands of its core constituency, the

Dalits. The upper castes will not hesitate to return to the Congress or BJP if their expectations of a share in both political power and economic gains are not fulfilled or, if these parties are able to revive themselves in UP. At the same time, with increasing political awareness, the Dalits may no longer be satisfied with self-respect, dignity and empowerment—which the party rightly claims as its achievement—and may also expect improvement in their material situation. By broadening its base, the BSP might find it difficult to retain its identity as a Dalit party/movement. Replicating the Dalit-Brahmin-Muslim model in other states maybe difficult, requiring very different strategies of mobilisation, as the distinct historical and socio-political features characteristic of UP may not exist elsewhere. If however, the BSP is able to meet these redoubtable challenges, such a development holds the possibility of introducing seminal changes in UP and perhaps, national politics.

The UP Experiment: Social Consensus and Inclusive Development

The victory of the BSP in the 2007 elections is not as sudden or as surprising as it seems. Both the BJP and the Congress performed badly in the 2002 State Assembly elections, the former gaining only 88 seats and 20.08 per cent of the votes and the latter a historic low of only 25 seats, its percentage of votes coming down to a single digit, 8.96. Again, in the by-elections to two Lok Sabha and 16 Assembly seats in mid-2005, the BJP won only one seat in the former; in the latter its vote share was a mere 11.7 per cent, just a little ahead of the Congress, which gained 8.5 per cent. This was a steep decline from the 21.7 per cent secured by the BJP (or by the candidates supported by it in a couple of seats) in these same seats in the 2002 Assembly elections. In short, the BJP's votes share nearly halved in only three years. As a result, what was a genuinely three-cornered fight between the BJP, the BSP and the SP in the 2002 Assembly elections underwent a radical change after the by-elections, with significant implications. The SP came to have a little over 41 per cent of the votes and the BSP almost 31 per cent, making it a two-horse contest with a 10 per cent gap.[1]

Equally important, since at least the 1996 State Assembly elections, the BSP had adopted the strategy of giving a large number of tickets to non-Dalits, including the upper castes. Then, in 2007, in the new political situation, it attempted to gain the support of the twice-born castes—Thakurs, Vaishya and the Brahmins—by approaching and mobilising them directly. The party

1. *The Times of India*, New Delhi, 11 June 2005.

held numerous *sammelans* seeking their votes, in which Mayawati's earlier anti-upper caste speeches were conspicuous by their absence and a more inclusive developmental agenda was put forward. With this new strategy, the BSP successfully created a winning Dalit-Brahmin-Muslim combine across the state.[2] At the same time, the victory in UP is not merely a result of an anti-incumbency wave against the Mulayam Singh government or of caste-based adjustments. Unlike most leaders, Mayawati realised the limits of caste-based divisions and politics. While most parties thrived on these divisions, such primordial loyalties, having reached a peak, began to decline in UP from the mid-1990s, necessitating mobilisation on issues of development and order. Thus, the decline of the national parties and the BSP's new social engineering strategy, together with the emphasis on inclusive development and law and order—which Mulayam Singh Yadav was perceived as having failed to provide[3] —paid off handsomely for the BSP. Meticulous planning of this strategy and its early implementation that began at least two years prior to the elections was an important factor in this success.[4]

However, this success does not mean that the BSP's position in UP is impregnable. The party leadership faces two closely related challenges: maintaining the Dalit-Brahmin-Muslim social consensus and providing an inclusive model of development. Analysis of the results of the UP elections show that the BSP increased its vote share from 23.0 per cent in 2002 to a formidable 30.45 per cent and obtained 206 seats out of 402. (Appendix Table A-1.1). However, it is important to realise that the SP has retained its social base, getting 25.43 per cent of votes that is almost the same as 25.37 per cent in 2002 and 21.8 per cent in 1996. The reason it obtained about 46 seats less is because the BSP was able to consolidate the anti-SP vote. The BSP's gain of almost 8 per cent was at the expense of the BJP that lost over 3 per cent and to a lesser extent the Congress, which experienced a decline of half a per cent.[5] What is significant is that the BSP won seats in the extreme western and eastern regions of the state, where it did not have much support and had long been the SP strongholds. It hence extended its support base beyond its traditional regions of Bundelkhand and East UP. Here, it must be acknowledged that its social engineering formula played a central role.

2. For details see Pai, 2007.
3. On the issue of law and order, see Pai, 2007(a).
4. On this aspect, see *Frontline*, May 4, 2007.
5. The Times of India (2007). "BSP mops up anti-SP Vote", *The Times of India*. New Delhi, May 12.

More important than electoral patterns is the seminal question: whether there is a new social consensus between the Dalits and the Brahmins, or is it merely a mobilisational strategy that has succeeded in the prevailing political situation. The success of the BSP has always been its knack for crafting new strategies suited to the rapidly changing politics of UP. Brahmins constitute 8 per cent of the state population and account for 10 to 20 per cent of the votes in as many as 40 of the 80 Lok Sabha constituencies (Ibid.). The direct oppressors of the Dalits (mainly landless labour) today are the OBCs (landowners in the countryside). The Brahmins on the other hand have moved away from land to professional jobs in urban areas. Thus, there is no direct antagonism between the two; the relationship has been described as resting on "technocratic rationality" (Kumar, 1996).

Traditionally, Brahmins in this conservative state have preferred the Congress and the BJP, and have not voted for lower caste parties. With the decline first of the Congress, which historically was the party that the Brahmins supported, and then the BJP in the early 2000s, they were in search once again of a party that they could support. The Brahmins found in the 1990s that the BJP–BSP coalitions do not provide stability and had little to offer to them. In a Virat Brahman Mahasammelan held at Bithauli village in Sitapur in May 1999, where they met to discuss their future political strategies, they bemoaned the fact that they no longer received contracts as in the past, which were now distributed by the BSP.[6] They are also unhappy because the backwards were given more importance in the party, as seen from the fact that no Brahmin has been made the chief minister of Uttar Pradesh, or even of Madhya Pradesh.

Moreover, Brahmins were not keen on joining the SP, as they regard it as a party dominated by the aggressive Yadavs and Thakurs in which their position would be weak. Rather, they feel that they would be in a better situation within the BSP to safeguard their position and attain posts of importance. The Brahmin–Dalit combination, they believe, can meet the challenge posed by the Yadav–Muslim bloc. They also point out that Dalits and Brahmins voted for the Congress party for many years. Mayawati also promised them tickets and cabinet positions. It is not easy for the Brahmins to join a party that once abused them as *manuvadi*, but nevertheless they were attracted by the importance that Mayawati is giving to their community in a bid to gain their support. They were impressed by the fact that Mayawati decided to

6. *Hindustan Times*, New Delhi, May 2, 1999.

bypass coalitions and instead opted for a direct mass-contact programme with the upper castes. Thus, the Dalit-Brahmin combine is a fragile partnership for political power and economic gains. If the latter do not get what they want, or if the BJP or Congress were to recover, they could move back into the comfort of their "natural" parties.

Following its success in the 2007 elections, the BSP launched a new strategy, titled "Mission Muslim", aimed at strengthening its minority support base (Ghildiyal, 2007). The party formed "Muslim Bhaichara" committees (to build brotherly relations with Muslims) in Agra, Meerut and Devipatan divisions and will soon extend them to other divisions. The committees consist of Dalit-Muslim members at the division, assembly and booth levels. To forge a bond, the members highlight the social marginalisation and exploitation by political parties of both the communities since Independence. The BSP is also keen to use this strategy in Maharashtra, where the community comprises a large number of migrants from UP (Gupta, 2007). It remains to be seen if the strategy is successful in keeping the Muslims away from the SP and the two new Muslim parties formed in UP prior to the elections.

To a great extent, maintaining the Dalit-Brahmin-Muslim alliance will depend on how far the BSP is able to fulfil the expectations of the different sections of the electorate that has voted it to power. The party will have to take care of both the specific developmental needs of the disadvantaged sections such as the Dalits, OBCs and Muslims, as well as the all-round and inclusive development that the state clearly requires. The former is not possible without the latter in the sharply deteriorating economy of the state: there can be little sectional development in a context of continuing underdevelopment. During the campaign, Mayawati was able to convince her Dalit followers that the BSP remained "their" party despite the new ties with the upper castes; it remains to be seen if she can continue to keep their faith by her actions while in power. The BSP will have to give up sectional Dalit-oriented programmes, the politics of symbolism and the populist programmes that it has constantly used in the past to gain votes and instead, concentrate on substantial economic development. In the given condition of the state, these are Herculean tasks even for a government with the clout of a majority.

The BSP Government may face difficulties in bringing about even a modicum of equitability in the stark imbalance between the lower and the upper castes' socio-economic situations, for it could lead to rivalry and conflict. The *Human Development Report of UP* (2003) shows this clearly: Dalits own hardly 8-10 per cent of land while the upper castes hold as much as between 55-65 per cent. Large sections of the Dalits are landless agricultural labourers or employed as low paid labour in the unorganised sector. Dalit literacy is low in the rural areas, particularly among women and this lack of education keeps them confined to the job sectors where the pay is pittance. In contrast, the upper castes have long formed the elite section both in terms of caste and class, and improved their position in the post-Independence period, reflected in their dominant presence in politics, higher reaches of the bureaucracy, academia and business. The Dalits would expect a BSP-headed government to bridge the gap between the two communities and bring the former into more prominent positions. BSP leader Sukhdev Singh Rajbhar, soon after the results were declared, said the aspirations of the Dalits would not manifest themselves as demands immediately, as they knew that this victory was only one step in the struggle of the marginalised sections to assert their rights and that their position will improve only over a long period of time.[7]

Some of Mayawati's early actions on assuming office indicate that she is trying both to work towards meeting the Dalits' expectations, while at the same time reassure its new supporters from the twice-born castes, so as to consolidate their support. She made it clear that the focus of her government will be the welfare of all sections of society not just the Dalit-Bahujans.[8] This is reflected in the caste composition of her ministry which allayed the apprehensions of upper caste BSP MLAs that the party may forget them after the elections. The ministry consists of eight Dalits, four Brahmins, four from the OBC and one each from the Muslim, Bania, Thakur and Bhumihar communities.[9] Efforts were made to improve the law and order situation. To win over industrialists and yet help disadvantaged groups, Mayawati offered a voluntary scheme of "incentives" and "facilities" in the form of tax and other rebates to the former for setting up units in UP if they reserve 30 per cent jobs for members of the SC, OBC, minorities and the "economically backward upper castes."[10] However, leading industrialists have rejected the offer, on the grounds that 'competence, not caste' is their prime concern when employing labour.

---

7. *Frontline*, June 1, 2007: 7.
8. See interview of Mayawati in *Frontline*, June 1, 2007: 8.
9. *The Times of India*, New Delhi, May 15, 2007.
10. Kalhans, Siddharth (2007). "Mayawati has new proposal: socio-economic engineering", *The Indian Express*, New Delhi, August 11.

The economic agenda announced by the government on assuming office also provides room for some cautious optimism, as it is radically different from that of the retributive social justice agenda of the past. On becoming Chief Minister, Mayawati in her speeches and pronouncements on economic policy has stressed on the need for removing the backwardness of the state through rapid all-round development of all social segments and regions. Soon after assuming office on July 20, 2007, Mayawati sought a special economic package of Rs. 80,000 crore for the 11th Plan period from the Centre for the development of the state. She spelled out that the priority areas: "rural development, agriculture, social development and infrastructure, making the state conducive for attracting investment."[11]

Mayawati's request to the Prime Minister in mid-2007 included a "Special Area Incentive Package" of Rs. 9,400 crore and Rs. 4,700 crore separately for developing infrastructure in two of the most backward regions of the state—Poorvanchal and Bundelkhand. She also sought Rs. 22,000 crore for the development of agriculture and allied sectors, Rs. 6,500 crore for rural development and another Rs. 13,300 crore for other important proposals for the integrated development of the state. She pointed out that the state had set a target of 10 per cent growth rate during the 11th Plan period (Ibid.). Similarly in the field of social welfare, Mayawati emphasised that her government had decided to bring down the number of people living below the poverty line by half during the 11th Plan. In contrast to her exclusionary policies of the past, she also requested the Centre to consider reservations and job quotas for the poor among the upper castes (Ibid.). Many of these policies were put forward keeping in mind the new constituency of "Sarvajan" that the BSP needs to cater to.

Only after months of negotiations with the Centre was Mayawati able to finally obtain Rs. 80, 000 crore for her state on February 18, 2008. This fund will not be in the form of a separate package, but a part of the overall resources being provided to UP under the 11th Plan.[12] The total amount available to the state under the 11th Plan will now be, according the PMO, Rs. 2,80,000 crore, amounting to 3.5 times the resources made available in the 10th Plan. The decision came despite the fact that the Planning Commission expert committee headed by B.K. Chaturvedi, which looked into Mayawati's

11. The Indian Express (2007). "Mayawati wants Rs. 80,000 crore to change the face of UP", *The Indian Express*. New Delhi, July 21.

12. The Indian Express (2008). "Maya gets her way, PM clears Rs. 80,000 crore", *The Indian Express*. New Delhi.

demands, observed that Rs. 1,81,000 crore resource for UP would need "major increase in the absorptive capacity, improvement in governance structures and major reform of the delivery system" (Ibid.). The committee further observed that "...if Rs. 80,000 crore as requested by the State Government is added to it, the total investment of Rs. 2,60,000 crore will certainly be unmanageable and clearly beyond the capacity of the state to spend" (Ibid.). Clearly, the funds have been given as part of a political deal because the announcement of the PMO came a month after Mayawati threatened to withdraw support to the Congress-led UPA Government if her demands were not met.

On completing six months in office in November 2007, Mayawati claimed that her government has put into place a three-pronged agenda of improving law and order and a slew of inclusive developmental as well as pro-poor policies.[13] On the law and order front, the government pointed out that the UP Anti-terror Act, 2007 had helped in removing land mafia, professional killers, liquor and drug mafia, kidnappers and extortionists responsible for causing social and economic harm to the state. The stringent action, it claimed, had brought down the crime rate. To ensure that the people develop confidence in the police, it was ordered that 23 per cent of all *thana* heads be appointed from the SC/ST, 27 per cent from backward categories including minorities and 50 per cent from other caste groups.

A number of policies, it is claimed, has been started for all-round development of the state, such as improvements in infrastructure and power supply;[14] assistance to cane-growing farmers who received Rs. 1593 crore from sugar mills and the cane price was fixed at Rs. 122.50. The earlier flagship programme of Social Justice for Dalits, the Ambedkar village programme has been revamped as a project for the upliftment of the entire village community, bringing in to its ambit 17,100 villages. Similarly, extra funds have been provided to *gram panchayats* for programmes for all, such as brick laying, covering drains, village roads, drinking water, toilets for schools, implementation of JRY, NREG and Indira Awas Yojana, etc.

At the same time, a series of pro-poor policies have been initiated, such as ensuring ration and programmes for minorities. Under the Kanshi Ram Urban

---

13. "Mayawati Ki Sarkar Ke Che Mah Ki Uplabhdiya is bath ki sacshi he", Information and Publicity Department, Government of UP, Lucknow. Advertisement in *The Times of India*, New Delhi, November 13, 2007.

14. 1000 km 8-lane expressways from Varanasi and Ballia to Noida for which 40,000 crore have been invested, a new international airport at Jevar, a new SEZ policy, investment in flood control, investment of Rs. 9209 crore and 7000 megawatts of additional electricity generated with more power houses to be built by the NTPC in the state.

Development Yojana, a number of programmes have begun to provide housing, roads, drinking water, sewage, cleanliness and employment. In key towns, a number of programmes for the poor including SC will provide housing, provision of essential services in slums, etc., at an expense of Rs. 3000 crore in five years. Encroachments on cultivable and housing land, given prior to 13 May 2007 to SC/ST, it is claimed, are being removed. Minimum daily wages for agricultural labour was raised to Rs. 100, increase in pensions granted, 88 thousand school teachers recruited, reservation in jobs in all industrial units supported by the government through various benefits of 10 per cent to SC, 10 per cent to other backwards and 10 per cent to upper caste poor will be provided.

Yet there has been some continuity with the past, both in terms of policy and rhetoric, as Mayawati cannot ignore her core constituency. An important example is the announcement in June 2007 of the decision to demolish the Gomti Nagar cricket stadium in Lucknow to replace it with a memorial to Ambedkar and other Dalit leaders. It is widely viewed as an attempt to remove doubts among Dalits as there are reports of uncomfortable signals from the ground after her increasing emphasis on Brahmins during the elections as well as during her first two months in power. Mayawati has made a request for an additional Rs. 23,000 crore as special assistance from the Centre for bringing the SC/STs, OBCs and religious minority communities into the mainstream. She has also supported the demand that reservations be extended to the private sector and put into the Ninth Schedule of the Constitution.

But most important is the decision announced on May 18, 2007 by the Chief Minister, at a meeting of senior administrative officers, to rigourously implement a law enacted in 2002 to ensure actual possession by Dalits of land allotted to them. Under it, District Magistrates are empowered to award six years imprisonment to those who forcibly occupy the *gram sabha* land alloted to SCs and others. The Chief Minister also directed the officials to ensure the possession of *gram sabha* land to all bona fide allottees within two months.[15] This order, if faithfully implemented, could lead to conflict and even violence in the state, as much of the land allotted to Dalits is already encroached upon by the upper/middle castes.

Another step that could prove an obstacle to improved economic governance in the state is the politics of vendetta. Soon after winning the election, Mayawati announced that "all illegal works taken up during the

15. *www.OutlookIndia.com,* May 19, 2007.

Samajwadi party regime will be probed." The government decided that all gun licences sanctioned during the previous regime would be examined; the State Law Commission and the State Council for Industrial Investment were scrapped; and many important decisions, such as the sugar and wheat purchase policy taken by the Mulayam Singh Government were overturned.[16] There are also reports that projects given to industrialists deemed close to the previous government, such as the Noida special zone, High-tech city, Dadri power project, among others, are being reviewed.[17] Mayawati also dissolved the Mulayam Government's UP Development Council headed by Amar Singh and has formed a new one along similar lines. The new body is likely to be headed by her close aide Satish Mishra.[18] Such decisions based on political considerations could delay private investment in the state, which is long overdue.

The continuing hostile relations between the BSP and the SP leadership is seen in the clashes between the cadres of the two parties, including the arrest of Mulayam's son, following an incident in Lucknow University during a protest for the restoration of student union polls, on January 9, 2008.[19] Opposition from the SP and its supporters, the Yadavs, who have a long history of ill-treating Dalits, could be an obstacle to the successful implementation of the agenda of the government. It is important to recall that the SP-BSP coalition in 1993 fell due to violent clashes across the state between the supporters of the two parties at the grassroot level, making such an alliance impossible in the future.

It remains to be seen if the funds will be fully utilised and these policies are put into action to satisfy the different sections of the targeted population. The BSP has won all the 3 Assembly and 2 Lok Sabha seats in the by-elections held in April 2008. The Congress and the SP, which had hoped that anti-incumbency had begun to make an impact on the new government, were badly defeated.[20] The BSP won the Muradnagar seat in Ghaziabad, even though the RLD had fielded a Muslim. Akbar Ahmed Dumpy won the Azamgarh seat. These victories show that the Muslims continue to prefer the BSP to the SP.

---

16. The Sunday Express (2007). "Mayawati in power, and not afraid to show it", *The Sunday Express*. New Delhi, June 2.

17. The Indian Express (2007). "Not just Anil, all SEZs and high-tech cities under review", *The Indian Express*. New Delhi, May 26.

18. The Indian Express (2007). "Maya aide set to head UP advisory council", *The Indian Express*. New Delhi, November 14.

19. The Times of India (2008). "Maya-Mulayam war turns ugly, *The Times of India*. New Delhi.

20. Ghildiyal, Subodh (2008). "Maya has opp on mat as BSP sweeps UP bypolls", *The Times of India*. New Delhi, April 17.

Similarly, Brahmin candidates won in Khalilabad and Bilgram constituency, demonstrating that the upper castes are still supporting the BSP. The SP has failed to win back social groups that did not support it in the last assembly polls: it lost Azamgarh and Khalilabad, both Yadav bastions, despite fielding Balram Yadav and Bhalchandra Yadav. The former, in fact, finished third. The results point to the BJP being squeezed out of the state. It obtained 1.35 per cent votes in Muradnagar, 3.5 per cent in Colonelganj, 5.03 per cent in Bilgram and lost the deposit in Khalilabad (Ibid.). While these victories maybe due to the continued weakness of the BJP and the Congress in UP, neither has the SP been able to re-establish its strong position as yet.

Moving Beyond Uttar Pradesh: Developing a Pan-Indian Identity

Following its victory, the BSP hopes to move beyond UP to establish a presence in other states in order to develop a pan-Indian identity. Much of this optimism is fuelled by two developments: the gradual increase of its vote share in a number of states since the late 1990s; and the importance of small parties increasing as national parties wane, leading to regionalisation of politics.

The BSP has been gradually increasing its vote share in a number of states over each election. In HP in the 2003 elections, it received only 0.7 per cent of the votes, while in 2007 it has risen to 7.26 per cent; in Uttarakhand, the rise has been from 10.93 per cent in 2002 to 11.76 in 2007; in Maharashtra, from 0.39 per cent to 4 per cent in 2007 and in MP, from 6.29 per cent in 1998 to 7.26 per cent in 2003. Only in Haryana, Punjab and Chhattisgarh has the vote share of the party dropped. Hoping to build upon bases that exist and spread elsewhere, Mayawati has already begun the task of mobilising in states across the country. She has held rallies in Himachal Pradesh, Madhya Pradesh, Rajasthan and Chhattisgarh, states lying in the Hindi belt that have a substantial section of Dalits and tribals. Her party members, particularly Satish Chandra Mishra, the architect of the UP victory, believe that the Dalit-Brahmin *bhaichara* experiment can be replicated in Madhya Pradesh, Rajasthan and parts of Punjab with some variations. It is pointed out that the leadership need not be with the Dalits in each state, it could be through either coalition with like-minded parties or by constructing a rainbow party, the aim being to advance a Dalit-Muslim-Brahmin combination. Moreover, it is argued that following the victory in UP, Dalits in all these states are moving away from mainstream parties and the BSP could mobilise their support (*Frontline*, June 1, 2007: 8).

In the non-Hindi belt, Mayawati has tried to move into states where a substantial Dalit population exists, or Dalit movements in the past have created high levels of political consciousness. In Maharashtra, with a politically aware Dalit population and the RPI divided into a number of factions, attempts began soon after the 2007 elections. The BSP inducted the Mahant (high priest) Sudhirdas of the Kalaram Temple at Nashik, who was told to replicate in Maharashtra the UP model of drawing upon the strength of all castes.[21] With the Khairlanji incident clearly pointing to the vacuum of leadership in Maharashtra, Mayawati, at a Mumbai rally in November 2007, attempted to reach out to the Dalits as well as the dominant Maratha caste, which has dominated the politics of the state in a bid to create a new coalition of forces. The BSP in October 2007 initiated meetings of the Brahmin community in Pune, Ratnagiri, Thane, Nashik, etc., where they can play a pivotal role and a Brahmin conclave has been planned in Pune.[22] Mayawati has also visited Tamil Nadu, Kerala and Andhra Pradesh where Dalit formations already exist and have experienced considerable mobilisation. The party has also decided to mobilise in Jammu and Kashmir, which has a large number of Dalits. She addressed a day-long rally on November 18, 2007 in Jammu and will be visiting other cities soon.

However, it will not be an easy task to replicate the UP model in other states. Each state has acquired its own distinct characteristics through its history and the developments in the post-Independence period, such as specific caste/class combinations, political patterns and different levels of economic development necessitating differential strategies of mobilisation. In the case of UP, there are distinct historical and structural conditions that have enabled the BSP to emerge in a brief period of a decade as a strong party.[23] Based on the earlier experience of the RPI, the state experienced a strong wave of Dalit assertion at the grass roots in the 1980s that was harnessed through sustained mobilisation by Kanshi Ram and later Mayawati. Following the formation of the party in 1985, Kanshi Ram mobilised the Dalits by forming first the BAMCEF, the DS-4 and later the BSP. As a result, by the early 1990s the BSP had successfully emerged as the party of the Dalits, replacing the Congress. During the 1990s Mayawati built a strong organisation and cadre, and used

21. *The Indian Express,* New Delhi, May 27, 2007.

22. Sonawane, Rakshit (2007). "BSP Applies UP Formula to Maharashtra", *The Indian Express,* New Delhi, October 15.

23. For details see Pai, 2002.

strategies suited to the rapidly changing political situation in the state that have contributed to the party winning a majority by 2007.

Unlike in UP, the Congress and BJP are not in decline in the other states of the Hindi heartland, except Bihar; a strong two-party system with turnover of power exists, in which the BSP is a 'Third Front' standing in the middle.[24] This is particularly true of Madhya Pradesh and Rajasthan, where in the previous State Assembly elections, neither of the two national parties were interested in an alliance with the BSP. Nor do the Congress and BJP in these states suffer from lack of leadership, as in the case of UP. Moreover, the upper castes in these states are not prepared to accept Dalit leadership and support a Dalit-led party, as they are still in a strong political position. Brahmins in UP were pushed into doing so as parties they traditionally supported were in total disarray and decline. The OBCs and middle castes in Madhya Pradesh and Rajasthan too would be averse to the rise of a Dalit party. In the former, the OBCs form a strong support base of the BJP with all Chief Ministers being drawn from among them. In the latter, the issue of reservation has played an important role in recent years. In Punjab, the Akali Dal is a strong identity-based party, which has the support of the Jat-Sikhs and other middle castes; the BSP made a mark in 1985, but has since witnessed major reverses.

Equally important, the BSP would have to undertake strong and concerted identity-based mobilisation in these states, for the party to strengthen its base among the Dalits. It has not done so as yet. This will be difficult in the changed circumstances with the party reaching out to the upper castes. The party would also have to build a strong organisation and particularly, local leadership that the BSP has not promoted in the past. In fact, prior to the 2003 elections in MP, Mayawati removed Phool Singh Baraiya who could have been instrumental in the party performing better in the state. This undermined the strong inroads made into the northern districts of the state during the 1990s. Brahmins, with whom the BSP hopes to form an alliance, are low in number and political position in states such as Maharashtra, Gujarat and Rajasthan. Forming an alliance with them would not yield much.

Moving beyond the Hindi belt will not be easy. The Dalit movement in these states will have to be qualitatively different, requiring political strategies different from those in UP. In Karnataka, the Dalit movement is more cultural than political, it will require a different pattern of mobilisation on the part

24. See Pai, 2004.

of the BSP to advance in the state (Charsley and Karanth, 1998). In fact, everywhere in the South, the emphasis has been on economic and cultural rather than political empowerment. Parties such as the DMK in Tamil Nadu and CPI(M) in Kerala have managed to improve the economic conditions of Dalits, in stark contrast to their condition in the northern belt, thanks to the Left rule. In Kerala, the process began in the colonial period itself with the mobilisation of the Ezhavas and was continued by the Left parties after Independence. As a recent study shows, human development indicators of the Tamil Nadu Dalits—health, education, nutrition and fertility—are much better than in UP (Mehrotra, 2007). The lesson from the Tamil Nadu experience is that technical interventions by the government are needed for improving human development among the poor. Social mobilisation alone cannot bring change. In Tamil Nadu, the Dalits have experienced economic empowerment and as the study shows, in a much shorter period than Kerala and in the post-Independence period (Ibid.). Yet at the same time Dalit parties in Tamil Nadu have not been able to advance electorally as they exist in the shadow of the Dravidian parties (Gorringe, 2005).

In Maharashtra, Dalit leaders within the RPI and outside, who consider themselves the legitimate heirs of the Ambedkarite legacy have been critical and even hostile to Mayawati's politics. Long divided into a number of factions, the leaders of the RPI, such as Ramdas Athavale and Prakash Ambedkar are apprehensive of Mayawati carving out a vote bank among their followers. Athavale and Namdeo Dhasal, leaders of the Dalit Panthers criticised Mayawati for not paying tribute to Ambedkar at Chaitabhoomi during her visit to Maharashtra in December 2007. The former also accused her of misleading the Dalits to strengthen the Hindutva brigade, as she has a history of forming alliances with the BJP. Hoping to turn the Buddhists against her, he called upon her to convert to Buddhism if she revered Ambedkar and wanted his followers to join her party.[25] Confronted with these hurdles, it remains to be seen if the BSP is able to advance in the southern states.

Despite these differences, recent years have seen a rising tide of aspirations among an emerging, newly educated and politically aware class of Dalits across the country, which could help the BSP in its search for a pan-Indian identity. This is seen in the demands for reservation of jobs in the private sector, so that they can share the fruits of liberalisation; expectations that the Central

---

25. The Indian Express (2007). "Maya under fire from Dalit leaders in Maharashtra", *The Indian Express*. New Delhi, December 1.

government will introduce diversity policies following the Bhopal Declaration of January 2002 and; the establishment of a Dalit Chamber of Commerce in Delhi, Western UP and Pune, in a bid to create Dalit entrepreneurs, etc. This new class looks up to the BSP everywhere and supports it in its ventures. At the same time, it could put pressure on the BSP to follow pro-Dalit policies, thereby jeopardising the Dalit-Brahmin alliance in UP.

Carving out a Role in National Politics

The victory of the BSP in the politically significant state of UP throws up new possibilities in national politics. Following the victory in UP, it is reported that Mayawati hopes to become the Prime Minister and her party organisation is already making preparations for the electoral campaign for the 2009 Lok Sabha elections. This may seem far-fetched, but at least one national daily newspaper editor in mid-2007 painted the possibility of such a scenario, in which a gradual breakdown of the UPA Government and the failure of the BJP to revive its organisation and build new alliances by 2009 would leave the field open for a non-Congress and non-BJP coalition of many, probably headed by Mayawati.[26]

Even if this does not happen, in the unstable and highly fragmented multi-party political system in which national parties no longer play a central role, small parties with a strong base in a few states can play a seminal role. The Congress party has been under pressure from the Left and other partners on many issues, particularly the nuclear deal. Its abilities of governance, as also of running a coalition have not been very impressive. The BJP, thrown into disarray and factional divisions with its defeat in 2004, is slowly recovering, as indicated by its victories in HP and Gujarat. Both have become cross-regional parties, i.e., parties based in regions competing for power at the Centre, since the mid-1990s (Pai, 1996). The Left parties that are limited to two states are facing a deep crisis in West Bengal.

Following the BSP's victory, it was initially felt that the party and the ruling Congress at the Centre would join hands, as they require each other's support. Congress president Sonia Gandhi's dinner meeting with Mayawati at the latter's residence in New Delhi was the high point in the relationship between the two. Pointing out that UP had suffered "huge losses" due to the "confrontationist attitude" of the previous BJP-led coalition government,

26. Gupta, Shekhar (2007). "Prime Minister Mayawati, backed by the comrades, no kidding", *The Indian Express*, New Delhi, July 22.

Mayawati had claimed to have inaugurated a new phase of cooperation and financial assistance for "balanced growth" of UP in key infrastructure areas. She was assured that the Central government would consider the following demands: setting up a new international airport at Noida and a national airport at Jewar near Aligarh; the inclusion of UP in the national Buddhist tourist circuit and; the speedy approval of pending projects under the Jawaharlal Nehru Renewal Mission.[27] In return, Mayawati made it plain that her party legislators would support the Congress candidate in the Presidential elections, which ensured the victory of Pratibha Patil. The dispute, among others, between UP and the Delhi government on the rules for plying buses in Delhi was soon settled. The UP governor T.V. Rajeshwar refused to grant permission for her prosecution in the Taj Corridor case and more recently, the Income Tax Appellate Tribunal has given her a clean chit in the disproportionate assets case putting the stamp of legitimacy on the huge amount of cash, properties and gifts given to her by her supporters for building the party.[28] She was also been given SPG security, raising her image to that of a national leader.

However, following the Gujarat elections and as we move closer to the next Lok Sabha elections, equations between the two parties are getting set to undergo a change. There is growing realisation that they have conflicting political interests for the Dalit vote bank. Mayawati has tried to mark out social policies distinct from that of the Congress, which will be a rival party in the 2009 polls. An example is her demand for job reservation for Dalits in the private sector, likely to be an important issue in the next national elections. The Congress in the run-up to the State Assembly elections of 2007 had refrained from criticising the BSP and targeted the SP for its failure of governance. But from January 2008, the Congress party is planning a series of agitational programmes against the policies of the BSP regime in UP. Starting with a rally at Jhansi on January 17, 2008, the party is working out a strategy to undertake agitational programmes on issues such as acquisition and compensation for farm land acquired for the Taj Expressway and the Ganga Expressway projects, as also over the drought in Bundelkhand region, which has witnessed a high incidence of suicide by farmers.[29] In the wake of the recent attack on the BSF camp at Rampur in December 2007, the Congress

27. The Hindu (2007). "Bitterness with Centre will end: Mayawati", *The Hindu*. New Delhi, May 27.

28. Thakur, Pradeep (2008). "Clean chit to Maya in assets case comes on top of other 'Concessions'", *The Times of India*, New Delhi, January 4.

29. Singh, D.K. (2008). "Gloves are out, Cong set to go after Mayawati", *The Indian Express*, New Delhi, January 2.

party has alleged that Mayawati is too busy electioneering in other states and spreading her message to pay attention to the developmental, law and order and security needs of her own state.

In this situation the major impact of the BSP's successes, in and outside her state, will be on the Congress, which has traditionally claimed to be the party that stood for the poor and the disadvantaged sections of society. This strategy is in keeping with Kanshi Ram's position in the late 1980s that the Congress was its "principal enemy" and that his Dalit party would rise at the expense of that party (Pai, 2002). The BSP leadership has already declared that it will contest all the seats in central and northern states due for polls in 2008, hoping to erode the two-party system that functions in these states and open up space for a third force (Rangarajan, 2008). The BSP has already played the role of a 'spoiler' for the Congress in many states, such as in Madhya Pradesh and Rajasthan in 2003 and more recently in Delhi, Gujarat and Himachal Pradesh in 2007.

In the Delhi local body elections early in 2007, the BSP won 17 seats.[30] In Gujarat, the BSP candidates' vote share ensured that 10 seats that could have gone to the Congress went to the BJP. In another 13 seats where the Congress and its ally, the NCP were well placed, the BSP drastically narrowed down their victory margins. In fact, in about 50 closely-contested seats, where the winning margin was less than 5000 votes, the BSP candidates played spoilsport for the Congress in as many as 18.[31] Similarly, in eight Himachal Pradesh constituencies the BSP cut into the Congress votes to ensure BJP's victory and raised its own percentage to 7.3 per cent.[32] The BSP hopes to repeat this game in Rajasthan, Madhya Pradesh, Chhattisgarh and Delhi, which will go to the polls in 2008.

Most important is the impact, the BSP could have, on equations in the Lok Sabha, post-2009 national elections. It hopes to capture seats in a number of states to displace smaller parties such as the Left, who together have 61 members, or the RJD, which has 23 MPs in the lower house (Rangarajan, 2008). The most important strategy could be to improve and deepen its position within UP itself, a state that sends a large contingent of MPs to the Lok Sabha. It is important to realise that even in 1991 the BSP had managed

30. *The Times of India,* New Delhi, December 29, 2007.

31. Tiwari, Ravish (2007). "Maya draws blank, gives Cong the blues", *The Indian Express,* New Delhi, December 24.

32. *The Times of India*, New Delhi, December 29, 2007

to get as much as one-tenth of the votes in the state. Taking the 2007 State Assembly election results as a lead for the coming Lok Sabha polls, it may be indicated that the party will bag 40-45 seats, affecting the power equations in the House. Some seats gained in the neighbouring states of the Hindi belt, particularly in Bundelkhand-Baghelkhand region, would give it a determining position (Ibid).

It is for this reason that Mayawati is attempting to build a pan-Indian Dalit image. Her birthday party, till now a major cultural event in Lucknow, symbolising the empowerment of Dalits, was to be given a "national" stature on January 15, 2008.[33] Earlier, celebrations were held in Lucknow and the day was celebrated as "arthik sahayog divas" when BSP office-bearers, MPs and MLAs gave to the party fund against targets fixed in advance. She has instructed her cadres that in 2008, it must be celebrated in a decentralised manner in every state at the district level. To give it a pro-poor image, she has instructed the cadres to assure that the contributions in cash should be distributed to the needy—widows, the handicapped and the poor. The attempt is to iconise Mayawati as a Dalit saviour, but the ground aim is to use the mobilisational technique of tapping this event for electoral gains.

Conclusion

Our analysis of the impact of the BSP victory in the 2007 State Assembly elections shows that political developments in the states have significant implications for national politics. The decline of the single party dominant system and emergence of a highly unstable and fragmented multi-party system has led to regionalisation of politics. The two national parties, the Congress and the BJP have gradually been reduced to region-based parties competing for power at the Centre, creating unstable coalition governments. In this scenario, the role of smaller parties has assumed significance beyond their size in national politics. This is particularly true of the BSP that represents a new political force based on democratisation in a key state like UP.

The chapter examined two significant goals of the BSP following its victory in UP, that is, first, establishing itself as a strong political force in UP and second, spreading to other states in order to construct a pan-Indian identity. In these tasks the BSP leadership faces formidable challenges and dilemmas. The party hopes to establish—both through mobilisation and more

33. The Times of India (2008). "Maya's birthday bash to go national", *The Times of India*. New Delhi, January 4.

inclusive developmental policies—a new party base similar to the erstwhile upper caste Dalit-Muslim combine that had enabled the Congress party to rule UP for a long time. This, it is argued, will allow the BSP to overcome its inability to capture power alone and yet build a social combine in which the Dalits are in a commanding position.

However, maintaining the social consensus of Dalit-Brahmin-Muslim established during the electoral campaign in UP is difficult. The longer-term relationship between the BSP and the upper castes remains tenuous. Until the 2007 elections the BSP had a very small proportion of the total upper caste vote in the state, most of which was in the hands of the BJP and the Congress. The main support base of the BSP remains the large majority of poor and illiterate Dalits residing in the rural areas, followed by a smaller number of the Backward Castes. Despite media reports, it is not clear how the Brahmins view the BSP. It is also not evident whether the BJP is a party in decline in UP, or whether it is merely undergoing a period of weakness because of internal divisions arising out of loss of power in the state and at the Centre. The recovery of the BJP or the Congress could lead to a return of the Brahmins to their traditional strongholds. This is a matter of honour for the Brahmins, who aim to safeguard their long held caste/class position of dominance in education, income and employment.

The BSP's election success on the all-inclusive platform of *Sarvajan* has raised Dalit eyebrows about its identity as a Dalit-based party/movement. It remains to be seen whether they will accept the attempt to bring the upper castes into the party on a large scale, as it might dilute the core Dalit spirit of the movement in UP. The constructed identity of Dalit is not homogeneous. There are significant sub-caste/class divisions within the party, held together by the electoral mobilisation of the BSP. Weakening of this identity could impact on the Dalit base of the BSP. Equally important is the small, educated middle class—intellectuals and tiny elite among the Dalits in UP and the country—who, having contributed to the success of the BSP, now harbour high aspirations and cannot be expected to like the concessions given to the upper castes.

What could really help the BSP to maintain its hard-won heterogeneous Dalit base, and yet retain the support of the upper castes and Muslims in UP would be its success in governance and economic development. Throughout the 1990s, UP experienced instability and financial breakdown due to short-lived coalition governments set up by parties more interested in strengthening their electoral base than in providing good governance. With the exhaustion of identity politics, the electorate expects better governance, its expectations having been raised by promises made by every party during the 2007 electoral campaign. While Mayawati has promised all-round development and adequate attention to all social segments, the challenge will be to simultaneously balance the demands of the upper castes and satisfy the hopes and aspirations of the Dalits. The basic challenge is to work out a way to 'equitably share' the gains of development. The priorities of the upper castes are resolving the debt crisis and attracting industrial investment to put the state back on the path of growth, as also to firmly enforce a firm rule of law and order. On the other hand, the priority for the underprivileged, particularly the vast majority of the subaltern Dalits in the countryside, is public investment in areas such as education, housing, agriculture and health. In the past, much of the economic policies of the BSP have been symbolic, populist sops for the Dalits. It will not work any more.

Equally difficult is the second area of challenge facing the BSP: expanding from a state party to a national one. It needs to make its presence felt in other states because, in an era of coalitions, parliamentary majority is manufactured in states. For this it needs to reproduce the Dalit-Brahmin-Muslim combine in other states. As our analysis has shown, politics in states such as Madhya Pradesh, Rajasthan or Punjab does not at present provide an easy opening to the BSP. For a vast mobilisation of the Dalits, minorities and the upper castes in these states, the party needs a well oiled organisational machinery and a strong leadership which the BSP, as an authoritarian party has so far neglected. The southern states require different strategies and patterns of mobilisation, as Dalit politics has taken a different trajectory here and there are already established Dalit parties that may make it difficult for the BSP to advance in this region. How far the BSP will succeed in its plan to play a central role in the Lok Sabha after the 2009 elections—for which it is already preparing—will depend on how strongly the the two national parties emerges from the polls. Much will depend on the performance of the BSP in the states going to the polls in 2008, namely Madhya Pradesh, Chhattisgarh and Delhi.

Nevertheless, if the BSP is successful in emerging as a broad-based party with a Dalit core, it could open a new chapter in UP and national politics. Historically, UP has been a state governed by broad, aggregative social alliances led by the upper castes/classes, first by the Congress up to the 1980s and then briefly by the BJP. But now, the fundamental difference is that the Dalits will occupy a predominant position in the governance structures. If the BSP is able to consolidate its position, it could lead to two seminal changes: more broad-based economic development with lower levels of populist politics, enabling UP to shed its status as an underdeveloped state and; a gradual secularisation of society and politics in a state that has been torn apart by identity politics. As for becoming a dominant national power, the party does faces enormous challenges, but if it does overcome them, it could carry the process of democratisation to its logical conclusion—a lower caste party ruling the country. Even now the BSP stands tall as an important player in national politics, whose trajectory is being keenly watched by all political observers.

References

Charsley, Simon and G.K. Karanth (eds.) (1998). *Challenging Untouchability: Dalit Initiative and Experience from Karnataka.* New Delhi: Sage Publishers. p.36.

Ghildiyal, Subodh (2007). "After Brahmins, BSP set to woo Muslims", *The Times of India*, New Delhi, July 30.

———. (2008). "Maya has opposition on mat as BSP sweeps UP bypolls", *The Times of India*, New Delhi, April 17.

Gorringe, Hugo (2005). *Dalit Movement and Democratization in Tamil Nadu.* New Delhi: Sage Publications.

Government of UP (2003). *Human Development Report: UP.* Planning Department.

Gupta, Smita (2007) "The Muslims of Uttar Pradesh", *Economic and Political Weekly* 42(23). June 09-June 15.

Kumar, Pradeep (1999). "Dalits and the BSP in UP Issues and Challenges", *Economic and Political Weekly*, XXXIV(14): 822-26, April 3.

Mehrotra, Santosh (2007). "Intersections between caste, health, and education: Why UP is not like Tamil Nadu", in Sudha Pai (ed.), *Political Process in UP: Identity, Governance and Economic Reforms*. New Delhi: Pearson/Longman.

Pai, Sudha (1996). "Transformation of the Indian party system: Lok Sabha Elections 1996", *Asian Survey* XXXIV: 1170-83. December.

———. (2002). "Dalit Assertion and the Unfinished Democratic Revolution: the BSP in Uttar Pradesh", in the Sage series *Cultural Subordination and the Dalit Challenge.* Vol. 3. New Delhi: Sage Publications.

———. (2004). "Choices Before the BSP", *Seminar* 534, February. *Beyond the Verdict.*

———. (2007). "From Dalit to Savarna: The Search for a New Social Constituency by the BSP", in Sudha Pai (ed.), *Political Process in UP: Identity, Governance and Economic Reforms*. New Delhi: Pearson/ Longman.

———. (2007a). "The Problem", *Seminar* 570. Special issue on UP, March. *Battleground UP.*

Ramakrishnan, Venkitesh (2007). "Dalit power", *Frontline*, June 1.

———. (2007a). "The new behenji", *Frontline*, May 4.

Rangarajan, Mahesh (2008). "Why Mayawati matters" *Seminar* 581, January, Annual Issue.

Appendix Table A-1.1

Seats and Vote Obtained by Parties in the UP State Assembly Elections 2007

Parties	*Seats Obtained*	*Vote Share*
Congress	22	8.47
BJP	50	17.00
SP	97	26.14
BSP	206	30.45
Independents and others	27	17.94

Source: Website of the Election Commission of India: *http://w.w.w.eci.gov.in*

2 New Social Consensus in UP

Problems and Possibilities

Hariraj Singh Tyagi

The imperative of social consensus or 'engineering' as one of the fundamentals of state rule has come to the fore in the popular thinking of Uttar Pradesh with the coming to power, after 15 long years, of a government with a clear majority in the 2007 Assembly elections. There is hope among intellectual and political circles that this could bring an end to the era of political uncertainty and indecision, and that the agenda of social unity, economic development and regional balance would be put back on the rails.

Does the importance of the elections lie solely in the fact that a single party won a majority in the State Assembly? Was it so momentous a victory that it would finally break the back of several thousand years of social divisions, economic and intellectual exploitation?

The main point to be kept in mind here is that the Indian social organisation is not based on social consensus, but on social divisions. In the Vedic period, we see a clear division between Aryans and non-Aryans. In the post-Aryan period emerged the *varnas*, which in course of time turned into rigid caste divisions. It resulted in an exploitative and inhuman social structure, which persists even today, though on a lesser degree.

As opposed to this, the founding fathers of independent India, as is the writ in the Constitution, envisaged the creation of a classless and casteless society through the process of adult franchise. But the sad truth is that the psyche of the common people remains enslaved, to a large extent, on the reality of this rigid caste division and the upper class's stranglehold on the establishment continues.

All the same, adult suffrage did awaken the first glimmer of political consciousness among the Dalits and backward classes. For the first time in the country's history, the upper classes and castes who had long been at the helm of affairs, were being challenged by the exploited and the deprived sections of the society. Within 20 years of Independence, it was clear that the 10-12 per cent elitist classes who had ruled the roost could not keep the underprivileged—50-plus per cent majority—out of power anymore.

In the 1990s, after the implementation of the Mandal Commission Report, there emerged a new power entity on the horizon. Dalits and backward classes belonging to the Muslim, Buddhist and Christian communities—that is, the underprivileged masses—started to feel 'a little more equal' to their Hindu high caste compatriots. They too started demanding reservations in the centres of power. The Sangh Parivar and the BJP tried to reverse this tide through 'Rath Yatras' and the 'Mandir Movement'.

For sometime they did succeed in fomenting a religious fervour and arresting this new tide but ultimately, the new consciousness of the Dalits and the backwards saw through the religion shenanigans. The secular movement of the deprived once again was seen marching relentlessly towards the centres of power.

Our Constitution envisages social unity and equality. However, the reality is that our social set-up is based on caste divisions. For hundreds of years several efforts, both individual and collective, were made to reform it. But there has never been an attempt or movement to demolish the unjust system completely. Buddha was the first to make a powerful and positive effort to fundamentally transform this social organisation. But it stood very little chance before the vested interests entrenched since ancient times. The old order continued to rule—with new distortions. However, the important thing to be noted here is that Buddha had launched this struggle on the slogan of *Bahujan Hitay, Bahujan Sukhay* (in the interests of the majority, for the happiness of the majority) because the remainder, constituting minority, were the ruling exploiters.

Dr. Ambedkar was well aware of this contradiction between the social structure and the ideas of the Constitution. Mahatma Gandhi and many leaders of the freedom movement also knew that not only the Hindu Dalits but also the minority communities had been the victims of thousand years of ruthless exploitation and had been deprived of social dignity and a place in the centre of power.

It was clear from the Montagu-Chelmsford Reforms of 1919 that, due to the pressures of the national movement, the country was moving towards self-rule through limited franchise. By this time, Dr. Ambedkar had established himself as the chief spokesman and leader of the Dalits. When

Montagu-Chelmsford Reforms were being discussed, Dr. Ambedkar, appearing before the Southborough Committee[1], had for the first time demanded adult franchise for the Dalits. He vehemently criticised the argument that only the rich and educated knew how to use their franchise. According to him, the use of franchise in itself was an educative process.

Ten years later, he reiterated his demand before the Simon Commission.

Top leaders of the national movement were also giving the matter a very serious thought. In the 1928 Calcutta Congress, Jawahar Lal Nehru in his report had proposed adult franchise for all including the Dalits. Mahatma Gandhi gave it his unstinted support.

In the Round Table Conference held in London, Mahatma Gandhi said that he was committed to the demand of the adult franchise because the hopes and aspirations of the Dalits could be fulfilled only through this process. It was during this conference that Mahatma Gandhi had a meeting with Prof. Harold Laski and other British intellectuals, where he reiterated that nothing less than adult franchise for all would satisfy him. He told these friends of India that adult franchise at one go would give the Dalits and backwards such a powerful democratic and political instrument that by using it they would get the dignity they deserved in society, as also their share in political power. It can be legitimately said that the right of adult franchise was included in the Constitution, framed under the leadership of Dr. Ambedkar and through the efforts of Mahatma Gandhi and Dr. Ambedkar. It was a very important revolutionary step, because in one great leap this powerful democratic weapon was placed in the hands of all women and men. Let us not forget that it took centuries for the English men to get this right and that the women got it only in 1928. American women got it just 8 years before that, in 1920.

After the Constitution came into being, the adult suffrage infused the underprivileged with a new energy and confidence to launch the struggle for social equality and participation in ruling the country. After the death of Dr. Ambedkar, this new awakening of the Dalits concretised in to the form of the Republican Party and Dalit Panther movement and a new equation started taking shape on the political horizon. By the fourth general election of 1967, this new equation had started a process that led to the end of upper caste predominance in the corridors of power.

---

1. Southborough Committee was a House of Commons sub-committee which was involved in preparing the Government of India Act, 1919. Among other questions, this Committee also looked into issues regarding adult franchise in India.

In the assassination of Mahatma Gandhi and the death of Dr. Ambedkar, the Dalit movement lost two of its most powerful leaders who, in their own balanced and dignified way, had awakened the Dalit consciousness. After this, the radical young elements of the Dalit movement came into the hands of the Republican Party and Dalit Panthers, who shaped it into an instrument of direct confrontation with the upper caste establishment. During the general elections held in 1962 and 1967, the Republican Party for the first time flexed its muscle and made a show of strength in the Hindi belt, raising venomous slogans against the upper castes.

Though nobody can doubt the radical leadership's commitment to the cause, it just did not have the balance, discipline and dignified maturity of Gandhi or Ambedkar, which are the pre-requisites for the progress and durability of any movement. The result was that by the mid-1970s most of the RPI leaders, greedy for power, joined hands with the Congress and the Dalit movement lost its edge.

With his extraordinary organising skills, Kanshi Ram gave a radical flavour to the Dalit consciousness and established it as a power centre in the UP politics. Using the Dalit mass power, he resorted to the politics of making and breaking alliances according to his convenience. Kanshi Ram's mantra was: "We don't need a strong government, we need a helpless one." He made no secret of his strategy: Both before making and after breaking the alliance, the Bahujan Samaj Party must emerge stronger than before. To sustain and radicalise the enthusiasm of the Dalits, he gave the slogan of "Tilak, Taraju and Talwar...", but once he became powerful enough, he gave up the aggressive slogan altogether. But it should be remembered that during the active period of Kanshi Ram's political life, Dalits, backwards and minorities—constituting the majority that is Bahujan—were always at the centre of his strategy. He believed that the stronger the Bahujan alliance became, the weaker would be the upper caste's stranglehold on power. And finally, disappointed and dejected, the upper caste would accept the leadership of the Bahujan just to save their share of power. With this belief and strategy, in alliance with Mulayam Singh's Samajwadi Party, they contested the elections and won. For the first time, a Bahujan government was formed in UP. This inspired, enthused and re-energised the movement. It is unfortunate that when the Dalit movement was marching towards its goal, its supremo Kanshi Ram fell seriously ill. The leadership of the movement fell in to the lap of Kumari Mayawati who was not grounded in the political and historical background of this consciousness, of its intellectual commitment and ideological base. Her inexperience, broke the back of Dalit-backward alliance in an atmosphere of bitterness. Dalits belonging to minorities also parted company and joined hands with Mulayam Singh in large numbers, believing he was worthy of their trust.

It will be an illusion to believe that the governments that followed (between 1991 and 2007) were alliances. These governments were nothing more than a cabal of vested interests—groups of political individuals who, for the sake of their narrow personal and political ambitions and in order to escape the provisions of the anti-defection law, gave this unholy union the shape and name of a political party. The then BJP Chief Minister and the Speaker of the Assembly, in a show of shameless partisanship, gave all help and support to this opportunistic and unprincipled alliance. Between 1991 and 2007, only two alliances took place that could be considered political. The first was between the BSP and the BJP, based on the understanding that each would be in power for a period of 6 months, turn by turn. It broke down before 7 months had passed. The second was between Rashtriya Lok Dal and Samajwadi Party, which managed to last 'all of' two and a half years.

It needs to be noted that, riding on the strength of Bahujan Samaj, Mayawati ascended to the chief ministership thrice and thereby damaged the organisations of upper castes, a minority class in the society. She got either the Congress or the BJP support, but in the bargain, both the parties lost big chunks of their mass base. It is in this period that, just to stay in power, Mayawati placated the BJP to the extent that in 2002 Assembly elections, she went all the way to Gujarat to canvass votes for Narendra Modi. Her greed for power seriously dented the great alliance of Bahujans. This process gradually weakened her and she desperately started wooing small groups of upper caste political animals.

Dissatisfied with this strategy of hers, the massive alliance of Bahujans disintegrated. One segment, the backwards and minority community, distanced itself from her and joined hands with Mulayam Singh. Although Mulayam Singh has been dislodged from power, he is still a very powerful alternative to Mayawati. If Mulayam Singh learns from the lessons of defeat and regains the energy he used to have, there could be a sea change in the political scene. The Ballia parliamentary by-election could be the pointer to what may come, but the time is not ripe for any predictions.

Nonetheless, I would like to emphasise the fact that Mayawati managed to bring together disparate and desperate groups not only in the Assembly, as was done earlier, but also outside it in the 2007 elections. She won over a large number of the upper castes to her alliance. These were the elements who were feeling ignored by their parties or were losing one election after another. By extending her solid vote bank to them, she gave them another lease of life to make a comeback.

The alliance attracted even the neutral voters who had become disenchanted with Congress and BJP because of the near total lawlessness and corruption during the Samajwadi Party rule. Importantly, though the strategy gave Mayawati a clear majority, the Samajwadi Party also won more votes than before. One reason for this was that, though Samajwadi Party supporters were unhappy with its governance and also knew the reasons for the shoddy performance, they somehow still had some faith in Mulayam Singh and perhaps, they still do.

Mayawati may have won, but in the process she has taken much of the zest out of the revolutionary movement. It has since then become sluggish. Kanshi Ram and hundreds of his comrades had worked hard to give the movement a steady momentum, taking it to newer heights. Mayawati came to this movement during its last glorious phase. She is certainly not its creator or its fount of inspiration. In this majority rule of hers, all programmes of Dalit upliftment have slowed down and in some cases, have even become defunct. Incidents of atrocities against Dalits have gone up. According to government statistics, incidents of Dalit oppression has doubled since the end of Mulayam's rule. The government's argument is that during Mulayam's rule such incidents were suppressed, but now they are all registered and suitable action is taken.

With the clarion call of "Bahujan Hitay Bahujan Sukhay", Dr. Ambedkar and Kanshi Ram generated a revolution that aimed at demolishing the rotten caste-class ridden system. Mayawati replaced the "Bahujan Hitay Bahujan Sukhay" call with "Sarvajan Hitay, Sarvajan Sukhay". This is a deceptive and dishonest slogan and by using it she might have secured a majority in connivance with the upper caste, but who can ignore the ugly reality that these very castes and classes look down upon Dalits and backwards with utter contempt and believe in keeping them at a safe distance? Mayawati has forgotten that the Dalit movement is seeded in Buddha's teachings, rooted in Dr. Ambedkar's crusade and grew to be a large strong banyan tree because of

Kashi Ram's long, patient struggle and nurturing. It is too strong for Mayawati to wish it away.

It is a basic political principle that a party which deviates from its fundamental values, original ideology, principles and programmes and resorts to opportunism cannot last long. The Congress and the BJP in UP are the prime examples.

The pressure this 'social alliance' or engineering has put on Mayawati can be seen from the fact that: incidents of oppression against them has increased since she came to power; the implementation figures of SC/ST Act is negligible; and the campaign to remove encroachment on land allotted to Dalits has practically failed. Programmes of Dalit upliftment and empowerment have given way to erection of statues and construction of parks. How much pressure this opportunistic social alliance is exerting on Mayawati can be gauged from the fact that, despite the announcement to put up a statue of Perriar, who is one of the most powerful symbols of Dalit consciousness, she has not been able to do so. Not only this, she has issued a government order which has banned statues, photographs and banners of Perriar and the publication of his thoughts through pamphlets anywhere in the state. According to her, Perriar is a great leader of the South, but he has no relevance in the North. Her excuse boils to narrow regionalism and goes against the spirit of a united India.

There is need to mention a sleazy fact about her social engineering. Mayawati brought in not just the upper caste losers, but also some election winners who were actually mafia men or were backroom political managers. BSP has not been able to get even a single person of stature who was a recognised worker or leader of any mass based organisation. Without them, there is nothing 'Sarvajan' (all people's) about this front. It is bereft of relevance and credibility.

Some leaders and political analysts see the rise of the Dalits and backwards as the cause of political instability that threatens the integrity of the nation. India's history and tradition belie any such apprehensions. The nation's unity is based on centuries-old emotional and spiritual integration, religious tolerance and cultural liberalism.

Events of the past 150 years support this contention. The freedom movement, a mass upsurge that encompassed the entire length and breadth of India strengthened the sentiment of national unity and the Indian Constitution gave this sentiment a positive and affirmative shape.

The Constitution guarantees all citizens equal opportunities and equal status. That these rights, post-Independence, were structurally put in place can be clearly seen from the way in which the Parliament and Assemblies functioned, Presidents and Vice Presidents were elected, ministries at the Centre and the states were formed, the way judiciary and armed forces functioned, and the way All India Services were reorganised and personnel for them were selected.

The Constitution allows for a one market economy in the country with one currency, and a non-discriminatory single trade and tariff system for all states. The importance of one-market-one-currency in a country of sub-continental size like India can be gauged by the fact that it has taken Europe almost four decades to follow suit with its ECM and the euro.

The rapid industrialisation, the technology revolution with its TV, computers and e-media, as also the elite institutes for learning business, science and engineering is turning India in to a storehouse of skilled and highly skilled workforce. Above all, students, peasants and trade union movements and organisations are playing a highly commendable role in demolishing the walls of sectarian regionalism. Hundreds of small and big cities and towns like Kolkata, Mumbai, Hyderabad, Bengaluru, Jamshedpur, Ranchi, Bhilai, Noida and Gurgaon have become hubs of industries and educational institutions. Here we find a happy mixture of various languages, religions and customs of people from different regions. And in this potpourri, there may well be brewing the culture of togetherness, which is the essence of national unity.

This chapter, one hopes, has amply shown that the awakening of the underprivileged classes—the Dalits, the backward and minority populations—and their struggle for a rightful place in society and equal share of power, all through democratic means, can never be the cause of national disintegration. The most fundamental elements of our nation—its geography and history—guarantee this. Its liberal traditions, composite cultural heritage, our integral mentality towards regional, religious and related diversities, as also the teachings from Buddha to Gandhi, the values of oneness instilled by the freedom movement, our democracy based on adult franchise *et al.,* are the surest guarantees against any disintegrating force.

3 From Contract to Consensus

UP's Political Predicament

Salil Misra

The thesis which holds that a new social consensus is growing in Uttar Pradesh, as a result of the assembly elections of 2007, is vastly exaggerated and a little premature. This is not to say that the social and ideological raw material that can create conditions for a new social consensus does not exist or is inactive. The point is that the results of an election are not an adequate indication of any such consensus. At best, they indicate tactical political shifts, not lasting politico-social alliances. What happened in the last elections is best understood as an episode. Episodes do not necessarily constitute 'trends'; they can also be aberrations.

I am a student of history and my research on UP is confined to the pre-1947 period and this is not my area. So I will examine this question of emerging new social consensus more in the light of certain abstract principles and not with any information available with me, as I think these principles will help us put things in a perspective. I would like to approach the belief in or the notion about an emerging new social consensus as some kind of a thesis. Let us look at it as a thesis and let us look at it without any kind of prejudice either way, for or against. The thesis may get validated with the help of data, available trends and logic or, on the other hand, these may turn out to have merely an episodic significance. Besides, an episode is often more of an aberration, in which the pre-points and the post-points can be joined together, so that the aberration ceases to have any long-term impact.

There are three important questions regarding this consensus thesis. Firstly, what are its political implications? Secondly, how did this situation deemed a potential for consensus, come about? And thirdly, an even more fundamental question is: has such a situation really come about? Does the conceptual claim of the thesis have enough empirical justification to state definitely that some kind of a consensus is in the making? It is quite clear that these three questions do not have all the answers that can sustain themselves.

I will go back to the pre-1947 period in UP and explore some unusual, out-of-the-hat kind of electoral alliances to examine the circumstances in which these alliances materialised and the fate that they met. Let me pick up two instances from the two general elections that we had prior to 1947—one in 1937 and one in 1946. The one in 1937 was about UP's Muslim landlords. These landlords had, since the 19th century, been opposed to the Congress, democratisation and the creation of representative institutions. But when these institutions were created with a substantial franchise, the landlords had no choice but to enter the electoral field. Being Muslims, they first found it convenient to join the Muslim League or to have some kind of an alliance with it, so as to win in the election. But that, for some reason, did not work. Therefore, they joined up with Hindu landlords to create a separate political platform of big landlords and formed the 'National Agriculturist Party'. Up till then, it was fine, seeing as how their class interests had brought them altogether. But what complicated the plot was that these Hindu landlords decided to form an alliance with the totally communal Hindu Sabha organisation. Many of the Muslim landlords, who still had some kind of connections with the Muslim League were faced with a dilemma. What were they to do about being allied to an openly communal Hindu entity? It did not take them long to come to terms with their religious conscience and decide to continue in the alliance—a classic example of class ties (read materialistic interests) overriding the communal divide. But the alliance was short-lived. They were routed at the elections, the alliance collapsed, the party disintegrated and the Muslim and the Hindu landlords each went conveniently back to their respective communal organisations—the Muslim League and the Hindu Sabha. That was the last one ever heard of the National Agriculturist Party.

In the second instance, the next general election in 1946, the state was witness to an even more unusual combination. This was not a formal alliance but a triangle of understanding amongst the Communist Party of India, Ambedkar's Scheduled Caste Federation and the Muslim League. They formed an informal alliance against the Congress. If in 1937 it was a case of clashing class and communal interests, this time caste also came into the picture. This is how it happened. In March 1946, there was a political riot in Kanpur with the Congress on one side and Communists, Muslim Leaguers and Ambedkarites on the other, fighting a fierce battle on the road. It was very like a communal riot, except that there were Muslims and Hindus on both sides of the battle lines. Fifteen people were killed and 70 injured. A mosque and a gurudwara were burnt down. Curfew was imposed and the army called out. Nobody knew who burnt down the mosque. Muslim League tried to discredit the Congress Muslims by blaming them; the Congress said that the Muslim Leaguers did it because the mosque sympathised with the Congress Muslims. In any case, the fragile and fluid alliance melted away immediately after the elections. I am not trying to argue that such loose alliances of disparate elements that did not materialise then will not survive now. All that I am saying is that the new alliances, new alignments which we are trying to call a consensus are not entirely unique or unprecedented. Other instances of this kind are there and it would be instructive to see what kind of a fate they met.

So, it is clear that there is nothing new about electoral misalliances in UP's political history, both in the pre- and the post-Independence periods. Groups that had nothing in common with each other were able to form electoral alliances. Most of them collapsed shortly after the elections. Indeed, these alliances across classes, communities, factions and ideologies have not been uncommon in India's electoral history. Quite often they have resulted merely in the rotation of social personnel, without seriously affecting the socio-political profile of the country. This chapter will go into details of some of these alliances and their fate.

There is a well known formula Sir Henry Maine has given us regarding the generic transformation of societies from: pre-modern to modern; agrarian to industrial; old to new type; and pre-scientific to scientific. He calls it the transition from status to contract, from the medieval type of status societies to modern type of contractual societies where contracts take place between individuals. I feel and this is a completely free floating idea which when applied to modern UP, it would have to be modified a little so as to indicate, not exactly a transition from status to contract, but more a co-existence of the two. This implies that, whereas status has not diminished significantly from the state's political and social life, contract certainly has made an entry into its politics. As a result, different groups and communities (not individuals) enter into multiple political contracts with each other. But these contracts do not really diminish status in any significant way, as contracts are supposed to. The status has somehow bracketed itself off or rather insulated itself so as not to be affected by the nature of the contract. Status groups have become deeply internalised, because they are not being given due recognition any more, thereby making the group highly self-conscious, inward-looking. Given its vested interests, the group has every intention of maintaining its status by very consciously believing in it, even if others don't. Such an internalised concentration of status instead of dilution would render any kind of social consensus somewhat difficult to achieve.

Why has status proved to be so resistant and so immune to contract? That is the question we need to explore. As the United Provinces of the Raj became Uttar Pradesh with Independence, it retained most of the elements of the electoral processes, but also underwent certain changes in its electoral life. The building blocks of UP's post politico-electoral life were the upper castes, tenants or peasant castes (later designated as OBCs), scheduled castes (later designated as Dalits and Muslims). These building blocks retained much of their internal coherence, but became much more mobile as the groups started to flit from one political formation to another. In other words, any political dilution or dissolution of these categories did not exist internally, but they lost their fixity and began to float around into different political and ideological formations. To take two examples, the peasant castes and the scheduled castes rallied behind the Congress in a very big way in the 30s and the 40s. The Congress won 15 out of 20 seats reserved for scheduled castes in 1937 and it won all the 20 seats in 1946, even when a Scheduled Caste Federation had come into being. But in the 60s, 70s and 80s, these groups left the Congress and relocated themselves into different political formations. This mobility occurred without any diffusion of these categories. Muslims, on the other hand, were traditionally not with the Congress and that again can be demonstrated for the 30s and the 40s. They were not with the Congress before Independence, but started to come into the party in the late 40s, 50s and 60s, with the result that the Congress acquired a substantial Muslim base, but in the 70s they started to move out. So, mobility has been of a group faction or caste and community kind and not individual. One can see that UP's politics is actually a story of multiple factions and various identities associated with these factions floating in and out of different political and ideological formations. In this process, no dilution and diffusion of identities has occurred, which is a necessary factor for formulating a consensus thesis. At the same time, there has also been no fixity or stable alliance between identities and political groups. So no political party can be very sure of the political allegiance of any particular group and I think, this is going to be applicable to BSP in times to come. No fixity, yet no dilution—that has been the paradox of UP's political life.

To sum up, any meaningful social consensus would require, among others, three pre-conditions. One, a marriage between political alliance and a social alliance. Let us not assume that a political alliance necessarily translates into a social alliance. The SP-BSP alliance of the 90s was short-lived because it was a political alliance without any accompanying social alliance. Two, a process of mobility is necessary, not just across factions and identities, but also within the factions and identities, so that their boundary walls crumble down. Three, there should be enough tenacity and resilience in political contracts so as to be able to undermine status. So far, there is little evidence to suggest that any of these processes are underway in UP's political life.

Basically, all I have done is to offer a framework of how the thesis of social consensus can and should be tested. I am personally not in a position to say more because we do not have enough information to test it and say anything definitive, but I think the framework is there, in the light of which this thesis should and must be tested.

4 The New Consensus Needs a Socio-Political Ideology

Venkitesh Ramakrishnan

The premise of this presentation is on short-term and the immediate socio-political trends and developments in Uttar Pradesh but the projection it seeks to make is essentially medium- and long-term. Broadly speaking, the politics of this state in the last half a decade, more specifically the period between 2004 and 2007, have been dominated by political and organisational initiatives of the Bahujan Samaj Party (BSP), which successfully advanced the concept of Dalit-Brahmin *bhaichara* (Dalit-Brahmin brotherhood) in manifest forms and through manifold means. The concept was taken forward as an effective campaign slogan, as a mass mobilisation tool and finally as a potent election strategy. This combination and the political practice that it represented led the BSP to the phenomenal election success of 2007.

But even though the concept of Dalit-Brahmin *bhaichara* succeeded as a mass mobilisation tool and election strategy, whether it would have a lasting impact at the societal level did not, at that time, evoke an affirmative answer. Indeed, the period immediately following the sensational (almost heady) election victory had shown that the "brotherhood" was far from becoming a cemented part of the social fabric of the country's most populous state. The period immediately following the elections were marked by several instances where sections of the Dalit communities were asserting their Dalit position, giving no thought at all to the *bhaichara* concept. At the same time, significant segments of the Brahmin community too, in spite of being party to the political success along with the BSP, were not really going along with the *bhaichara* deal. I had carried out a fairly detailed field study, as part of the ORF project itself, during and after the 2007 elections. The study had revealed that in scores of the villages in the districts of Baghpat, Muzaffarnagar and Meerut, the dominating upper caste denizens refused to allow the Dalits to occupy the *patta* land allotted to them by the government. Repeated orders by the official machinery, even from the Chief Minister's office to the district magistrates failed to make any impact. There are no indications that the situation has dramatically changed in the period following the field study, which was made six months after the Mayawati-led BSP government came to power. In other words, there have been no political, organisational or social initiatives or administrative steps that have produced any significant change in the social imbalance.

In many ways, this whole process—that of the BSP's *bhaichara* concept succeeding as an election tool but not as an instrument of social reform—is in keeping with the historical processes through which the BSP has reached the present stage of its political activism and strategy. Right from the late 1980s to the early 1990s, when the BSP emerged as a significant force and up to the 1993 elections, when the BSP aligned with the Mulayam Singh Yadav-led Samajwadi Party (SP)—which is essentially an intermediate caste party—Kanshi Ram, the BSP's founder used to emphasise on two aspects of the party's political practice. One of them was about the BSP's lack of belief in ideology-oriented political action. He held that capturing power by itself would bring in far reaching reforms in the society and that there was no need to take concrete ideological positions on any matter. From issues ranging from land reforms to reservations, the party had no stated ideological position. This was in direct contrast to the Left parties, which carried out all their political activity laying great emphasis on ideological positions on issues like land reforms. The question of land reforms was not an agitational plank for the BSP. Even the question of reservation was not an important plank. Kanshi Ram's political plank was essentially about one idea; changing the balance and structure of power in the country. He had this catchy way of explaining this point with a twirl of his pen. Holding it in a perpendicular position, he would say that this is the power structure of the country. Then he would hold the pen horizontally and say this is how the BSP wants the power structure to be. But he would add, to make it horizontal, one may have to first turn it upside down. The BSP's current political practice, apparently, was aimed at this upside down position, which ultimately would lead to a horizontal political structure. Put simply, the concept was that the Dalits, which he said was the *bahujan samaj*, the majority of the population, have to capture power and once that power is captured, everything else would follow. Then land reforms will happen, the social indices will improve and all other progress in different streams of society would start to happen.

Throughout the period Kanshi Ram advocated this 'power first' policy, political observers had expressed doubts about this kind of militant pursuit of power by itself being enough to change the situation on the ground. Practitioners of Marxist-Leninist philosophy and Left parties, who were considered to represent the struggling masses and the downtrodden, had said that this lack of ideology is not going to help the BSP to establish itself as a political power. But as it turned out, this 'power first' policy not only helped the BSP emerge as a big party but also changed the life situation of Dalits in large parts of Uttar Pradesh and in some parts of Punjab and Rajasthan. There is this famous case which is often quoted about a Dalit woman of Ambedkar Nagar district. After Mayawati's first ascent to power, along with the BJP, there was an attempt to rape this Dalit woman but she resisted aggressively and ended up doing the bobit on the upper caste assailant. At the police station, when asked how she had mustered the courage to take the drastic action, her reply was simple: Only because Mayawati had come to power.

This BSP inspired rise in morale and the development of courage to stand up against oppression is something that I had the occasion to witness throughout the salad years of the party. This rise of morale transformed the very social behaviour of a large number of Dalits. As a journalist, I have visited umpteen Dalit villages where, for many decades since 1952, the Dalits had been too frightened to go to the polling booth, but the emergence of the BSP finally gave them the courage to go and vote. This is especially true of several places in eastern and western UP. When Kanshi Ram passed away, I had this interaction with the 70-year old Daulat Ram, an agricultural labourer from Saharanpur who had taken a jeep load of people for their leader's funeral in Delhi. He described the change brought about by BSP and Kanshi Ram's politics on himself and the people of his village in one sentence. According to him but for Sahib (as Kanshi Ram was called by hundreds of BSP supporters) he and his friends would never have had the courage to hire a vehicle and travel outside the village. "Sahib showed us that we too have the right to make use of all the facilities like renting a jeep and taking it out of the village." This was the kind of fundamental change that an organisation like the BSP brought about, despite stating repeatedly that it does not have an ideology or that it is not an ideology-oriented organisation. What this shows is that the BSP's pursuit of power politics left a very significant impact at both the political and the social level, to the surprise of many a conventional political analyst. This is one aspect of the BSP's political action plan.

The other aspect often mentioned by Kanshi Ram in terms of his political practice was that it is easier for the *bahujan samaj* (the Dalit community) to socially and politically associate with the Brahmins who form the topmost layer of the caste hierarchy than with the intermediate castes who are lower than the Brahmins but higher than the Dalits in the caste spectrum. This is something that he used to repeat off and on in the late 1980s and early 1990s. Kanshi Ram's explanation was that caste conflict manifests itself in the most brutal and intense manner between the Dalits and the castes hierarchically immediately 'above' them. He held that the Brahmins and Dalits do not come into conflict in a direct manner in spite of the fact that the ancient Brahmins had visualised the entire social structure that Kanshi Ram used to oppose vociferously. This was the premise on which he broke his relationship with the Samajwadi Party—which had a Yadav-Muslim support base—and aligned with the BJP, saying that it is easier to work with a party that has an essentially upper caste thrust.

By any yardstick, Mayawati's Dalit-Brahmin *bhaichara* is only an extension of this premise advanced by Kanshi Ram. However, it is evident that Mayawati has taken this political premise beyond the realm of political parties and taken it into a social and political level, by virtually forging a social alliance between Dalits and Brahmins. So a comprehensive assessment of the BSP phenomenon would have it that, despite the disinclination to spell out an ideological position on very many issues of national importance, the party has not only made significant political gains but has also had a major social impact, even in the day-to-day lives of its core constituency, the Dalit people.

But the question now, after having reaped a major political victory by sewing up a momentous social coalition, is whether the BSP can continue with this political plan, which is essentially just a mobilisation strategy motivated by realpolitik concerns. A supplementary to it would be whether this realpolitik plan would succeed in the long run. Indeed, this is the question that seems to have come up within the echelons of the BSP itself after the 2007 victory, and at the moment there seem to be no answers. If one were to make an analysis on the basis of the first five by-elections held in UP, when the government was about to celebrate its first anniversary, one could make a case that the realpolitik plan is still working. But an overall analysis cannot be made on the basis of by-election results alone. For, political observers and journalists have increasingly started to notice, during the first year of the BSP government, a groundswell of vocal opinion aired mainly by intermediate castes and non-Brahmin upper castes against the party and its governance. And this vocal opinion essentially highlights the conflicts within the ruling dispensation and its governance, while catering to two different social groups with different emphasis in terms of social, political and economic interests. The vocal opinion points towards a kind of imbalance in governance while catering to the diverse interests of the two communities. Some measures of the government are perceived as providing discriminatory advantage to Dalits, while some others are being perceived as unduly favourable to Brahmins. Interestingly, this opinion is reflected within the two communities too. This development carries within it the possibility of a depletion of the BSP's core support base. Governance, administration and economic development could be the core areas through which the government could keep the Dalit-Brahmin coalition going but any depletion of its core constituency or core strength will ultimately make the BSP weaker and weaken its plans of emerging as a party of national stature.

It is this phenomenon, this inability to reconcile between the conflicting social, political and economic interests of the two communities at two different ends of caste and class hierarchy, that has given credence and relevance to the position that it is time the BSP evolved a clearly laid-out ideological positions on important social, political and economic questions. This ideological positioning would have to be such that it reasserts a predominantly pro-Dalit position. It would have to keep issues like land reforms and reservation policy at the core of this positioning.

II

Development of Uttar Pradesh: Performance and Prospects

5 Uttar Pradesh Economy

Past Performance and Future Challenges

Ajit Kumar Singh

Introduction

Uttar Pradesh played an important role in the polity and economy of the country in the pre-Independence days. It was known for its prosperous and hard working peasantry and was a major producer of food grains and horticultural crops. It had a large number of modern and traditional industries. Numerous sugar mills dotted the rural areas throughout the state. Kanpur was a major textile centre of the country. The state was known for its good educational institutions. Students from all over the country flocked to Universities of Allahabad, Lucknow, Aligarh and Benaras. Its per capita income was almost at par with that of the nation at the time of Independence. It was counted among the best administered state of the country. The state played a major part in the freedom struggle and threw up leaders of national and international stature.

For a long time after Independence UP remained a major force in the polity of the nation. With 80 MPs representing the state in Parliament, it could swing the political fortunes of the parties and the country. Till 1990, almost all the Prime Ministers of India came from Uttar Pradesh with the exception of the short tenures of Guljari Lal Nanda as interim Prime Minister and Morarji Desai. With the end of the supremacy of the Congress Party and increasing political fracture in the state polity, UP lost its political eminence after 1990.

But preceding its political downfall was the more dramatic economic decline of the state, which led to its being bracketed with other BIMARU states. Today, the very mention of the name Uttar Pradesh conjures up the image of a backward and slow moving state which is pulling down the growth of the country. Except for a brief spell during the 80s, its economic growth rate has consistently remained behind the national growth rate while its population has continued to grow uncontrolled above the national average. The result has been that the per capita income in the state, which was nearly at par with the national figure in 1951 has come down to almost half of the national figure and the gap is increasing. This gap in per capita state and national income is indicative of the lost opportunity. If UP had continued to grow even at the national average growth rate, which was rather modest for most of the planning period, its per capita income would have been double its present level and the poverty level far lower.

All the indicators of economic and social development for UP present a rather dismal and depressing picture: low per capita income, slow economic growth, high birth rates, widespread poverty, high infant and maternal mortality rates (IMR and MMR), low literacy especially among females, poor health outcomes, as also high incidence of child and women nutritional deficiency. In all these indicators UP ranks among the bottom 3-4 states among the major states of India. It invariably ranks at 14th or 15th on the lists of economic and social indicators, as numerous studies have shown (Table 5.1).

Table 5.1

Select Human Development Indicators for Uttar Pradesh and Other States

States	*IMR*	*Life Expectancy*	*Literacy Rate*		*Sex Ratio*	*Per Capita NSDP (Rs)*	*% Persons below Poverty Line*
			Total	*Female*	*0 to 6 yrs*		
	2005	*2003*	*2001*	*2001*	*2001*	*2003-04*	*2004-05*
Andhra Pradesh	57	63.7	61.11	51.17	978	21372	15.8
Assam	68	58.0	64.28	56.03	932	12821	19.7
Bihar	61	61.0	47.53	33.57	921	7319	41.4
Gujarat	54	63.5	69.97	58.6	921	26672	16.8
Haryana	60	65.4	68.59	56.31	861	29504	14.0
Karnataka	50	64.6	67.04	57.45	964	21238	25.0
Kerala	14	73.6	90.92	87.86	1,058	13722	15.0
Madhya Pradesh	76	57.1	64.11	50.28	920	14784	38.3
Maharashtra	36	66.4	77.27	67.51	922	13732	30.8
Orissa	75	58.7	63.61	50.97	972	12645	46.4
Punjab	44	68.6	69.95	63.55	874	28607	8.4
Rajasthan	68	61.3	61.03	44.34	922	15738	22.1
Tamil Nadu	37	65.4	73.47	64.55	986	23358	22.5
Uttar Pradesh	73	59.3	57.36	42.98	898	11534	32.8
Rank of UP	(13)	(12)	(14)	(14)	(13)	(14)	(12)
West Bengal	38	64.1	69.22	60.22	934	20548	24.7
India	58	62.7	65.38	54.16	933	20936	27.5

Source: Government of India, *Economic Survey (Annual)*, Ministry of Finance.

This poor economic performance has been despite the fact that UP is endowed with rich natural and human resources. The state is endowed with one of the most fertile land tract in the world with plenty of surface and underground water, abundance of rainfall and a farmer-friendly climate. It has large livestock resources. It has a vast source of cheap and unskilled labour as well as skilled and educated manpower. The state has been providing political leaders, bureaucrats and technocrats who have been manning and running the best institutions in the country. In short, UP is a state with great potential which remains largely unexploited.

It is high time that the people concerned with the state's development ponder over the factors that have led to the present state of affairs and suggest measures to take the state on a high growth path, at least to keep abreast of the national level. It is in this context that this chapter looks at the economic performance and the constraints on development in the state and offers suggestions for the road ahead.

Structure of UP Economy

The economy of UP is characterised by a number of features which one has to keep in mind while analysing its economic performance. The state is marked by low levels of urbanisation with hardly one-fifth of the population living in the towns and cities. The urbanisation level in the state is far lower than the national average and much below those in developed states like Maharashtra, Gujarat and Tamil Nadu where more than 40 per cent of the population are urbanites. Moreover, the pace of urbanisation has been slow and its economy not dynamic enough to absorb surplus labour from the rural areas.

Primarily an agrarian economy, two-thirds of its workforce is engaged in agriculture. The pace of structural shift in employment has been rather slow. The agricultural share in the state's income has been steadily coming down and presently stands at around one-third. Still, the dependence of the state economy on the agricultural sector is much greater than at the national level. Due to the rural orientation of its economy, the state is not able to share in the gains coming from the rapid growth of services and the manufacturing sector which are now the prime movers of growth. On the other hand, the excessive demographic pressure on land, leading to smaller and smaller holdings, combined with slow growth of non-agricultural employment is further increasing rural poverty.

Regional Disparities

Being a large state, UP suffers from highly unbalanced economic and social development among regions and districts. Presently, the state is divided into four economic regions, namely, western, central, eastern and Bundelkhand in the south. The first three regions fall in the fertile Gangetic plains which are well endowed with good soil and water resources, while Bundelkhand forms part of the dry central plateau region. The western region is more developed than the other regions and the eastern region is the most backward. Bundelkhand, located in the dry southern plateau is a geographically handicapped region with special problems. The central region falls in the middle category.

The eastern region and Bundelkhand are officially recognised as backward regions and are given special attention in development plans. The two regions suffer from lack of diversification of economy. The majority of population in the eastern as well as in Bundelkhand regions is dependent on agriculture for their livelihood, their numbers being 66 per cent of the main workers in the east and 70 per cent in Bundelkhand, as per the 2001 Census. The farmers in the two regions exist at subsistence level. More than 90 per cent area is under food grain crops. Productivity of all major crops is below the state average. Both the regions are industrially least developed. Economic growth is constrained by lack of infrastructure, particularly in the rural areas.

All the four economic regions also show considerable intra-regional variations at the district level. A recent study by the state's Planning Department has classified and ranked the districts, using 29 indicators to measure the composite development index of each district. The study revealed that out of the top 20 districts, as many as 15 were in the western region. On the other hand, among the bottom 20 districts, as many as 17 districts were in the east UP (Table 5.2).

The sharp imbalance in the regional development levels has led to demands for division of the state into 3 or 4 smaller states. Rashtriya Lok Dal has been demanding a separate Harit Pradesh consisting of western districts and similar demands have been made for a separate Bundelkhand, as also for east UP, but on a more muted note. The political support given by Mayawati's support for the state reorganisation demand has brought the issue more forcefully to the forefront.

Table 5.2

Ranking of Uttar Pradesh Districts according to Composite Level of Development (2005)

	First Quintile			*Second Quintile*	
1	Gautam Buddha Nagar	405.1	15	Muradabad	110.7
2	Ghaziabad	185.6	16	Bulandshahr	110.7
3	Meerut	149.5	17	Kanpur Dehat	107.0
4	Kanpur Nagar	141.4	18	Bareilly	106.8
5	Lucknow	136.7	19	Aligarh	105.7
6	Muzaffarnagar	125.1	20	Pilibhit	105.5
7	Bijnor	121.9	21	Sonbhadra	105.4
8	Saharanpur	119.4	22	Bagpat	104.8
9	Mathura	119.1	23	Farrukhabad	104.0
10	Agra	116.0	24	Etawah	102.7
11	Jyotiba Phule Nagar	114.6	25	Jalaun	101.6
12	Varanasi	114.3	26	Firozabad	101.5
13	Jhansi	113.8	27	Shahjahanpur	101.4
14	Rampur	113.4	28	Kannauj	100.6
	Third Quintile			*Fourth Quintile*	
29	Hathras	100.3	43	Fatehpur	88.5
30	Lakhimpur Kheri	98.7	44	Badaun	87.1
31	Mahoba	98.4	45	Rae Bareli	86.8
32	Auraiya	96.6	46	Unnao	86.7
33	Gorakhpur	95.6	47	Ballia	84.4
34	Allahabad	94.1	48	Basti	83.4
35	Faizabad	93.4	49	Pratapgarh	83.3
36	Mainpuri	92.9	50	Mirzapur	83.0
37	Barabanki	92.2	51	Kushinagar	82.6
38	Lalitpur	90.9	52	Ambedkarnagar	82.6
39	Sultanpur	90.7	53	Deoria	82.3
40	Hamirpur	90.7	54	Mau	81.6
41	Sitapur	90.1	55	Chandauli	81.4
42	Etah	89.8	56	Sant Rabidas Nagar	80.6
		Bottom Quintile			
57	Hardoi	79.8	64	Gonda	76.9
58	Bahraich	79.0	65	Jaunpur	76.9
59	Ghazipur	78.9	66	Kaushambi	76.9
60	Banda	78.8	67	Balrampur	73.5
61	Maharajganj	78.8	68	Chitrakoot	69.4
62	Siddharth Nagar	77.9	69	Sant Kabir Nagar	69.3
63	Azamgarh	77.0	70	Shrawasti	63.5

Source: Annual Plan 2006-07, Government of UP.

This issue cannot be discussed here at length but it appears to the author that, in its present monolithic form, UP is a politically and administratively unmanageable state. In fact, the State Reorganisation Commission had recommended the division of Uttar Pradesh into three separate political entities. The issue surely needs to be discussed in depth dispassionately. In fact, it is time to appoint another state reorganisation commission which may look at the whole picture rather than take piecemeal decisions.

Growth Performance

The state's economy has moved through four different stages of economic growth:

Period 1 (1951 to 1975)	:	Period of Economic Stagnation
Period II (1975 to 1990)	:	Period of Accelerated Growth
Period III (1990 to 2002)	:	Period of Deceleration
Period IV (2002 to 2007)	:	Period of Slow Recovery

During the first 25 years of economic planning, the growth was extremely low at around 2 to 2.5 per cent per annum which was lower than the state's population growth and of course, the national growth rate. The development rate picked up since the Fifth Plan period and caught up with the national growth rate in the Sixth and the Seventh Plan period (Table 5.3). The growth was largely agricultural, in the wake of the Green Revolution (Singh, 2000). Industries also showed high growth during this period. However, since the beginning of the 90s, growth rate in UP decelerated markedly and remained hardly around 3 per cent per annum. However, some acceleration has been seen in the recent period.

Low Plan Investments

The slow, fluctuating growth is directly linked to the low investment levels in the state. Being a poor state with a low tax-SDP ratio, the state revenue did not generate enough surplus for investment from its own sources. No major public sector project was started in UP either in the state sector or the central sector during the first two decades of planning. The flow of resources from the Centre through the mechanism of Finance Commissions as well as that of Planning Commission remained relatively low for UP in per capita terms. Some improvement in the flow of financial resources from the Centre took place during the 70s and the 80s but it was not adequate to overcome the long neglect of the past.

Table 5.3

Compound Annual Growth Rate of Total and Per Capita Income in Uttar Pradesh and India since 1951

Period	CAGR of Total Income (%)		CAGR of Per Capita Income (%)	
	Uttar Pradesh	India	Uttar Pradesh	India
1951-1956	2.0	3.6	0.5	1.7
1956-1961	1.9	4.0	0.3	1.9
1961-1966	1.6	2.2	-0.2	0.0
1966-1969	0.3	4.0	-1.5	1.8
1969-1974	2.3	3.3	0.4	1.1
1974-1979	5.7	5.3	3.3	2.9
1981-1985	3.9	4.9	1.5	2.7
1985-1990	5.7	5.8	3.3	3.6
1990-1992	3.1	2.5	1.1	0.4
1992-1997	3.2	6.8	1.4	4.9
1997-2002	3.1	5.3	1.0	3.3
2002-2005	3.7	6.7	1.6	4.9

Source: Plan Documents, Government of Uttar Pradesh.

The size of a state plan is an important indicator of public investment. Till mid-70s, plan investment in UP remained below 4 per cent of NSDP (Table 5.4). There was a visible improvement in the ratio of plan investment during the Fifth, Sixth and the Seventh Plan which is also reflected in the relatively faster economic growth the state experienced during this period. However, the state was caught in the grip of an ever deepening fiscal crisis from the late eighties (Singh, 2007). The levels of revenue deficit and gross fiscal deficit remained high till recently. The mounting revenue expenditure of the state government left little amount to be devoted to capital expenditure. Thus, we find that the ratio of plan expenditure to NSDP dipped significantly in the 90s and capital expenditure of the government came down to around 5-6 per cent of its total expenditure. The decline in public investment was reflected in the deceleration in the growth rate of the state economy.

Poor Investment Climate

Not only were the public investments low but the state government also failed to create a favourable investment climate that would attract private investment on a large scale to boost the state economy. By a rough reckoning, investment levels in UP are around 15-16 per cent of GSDP whereas at the national level, this rate is more than double. No wonder the growth rates in UP economy are much lower than that of India as a whole.

Table 5.4

Plan Expenditure in Uttar Pradesh under Five Year Plans

Period	*Plan Expenditure (Rs. Crores)*	*Plan Expenditure as Per cent of NSDP*
	Five Year Plans	
1951-1956	153	2.05
1956-1961	233	2.66
1961-1966	561	4.53
1966-1969	455	3.86
1969-1974	1166	4.69
1974-1979	2909	7.01
1979-1985	7356	7.62
1985-1990	11949	7.44
1990-1992	7772	7.28
1992-1997	21683	4.73
1997-2002	28386	3.84
	Annual Plans	
1997-98	5033	3.66
1998-99	5648	3.67
1999-2000	5843	3.53
2000-01	5897	3.40
2001-02	5965	3.16
2002-03	6702	3.30
2003-04	7242	3.33
2004-05	10205	4.53
2005-06 (RE)	17331	6.82
2006-07 (BE)	22106	8.20

Note: Percentages from 1997-98 are in terms of GSDP.

Source: Plan Documents, Government of Uttar Pradesh.

All available information indicates that investment activity in UP is indeed very low. UP's share in total proposed investment, through IEMs in the country between August 1991 and November 2007 was a meagre 5.32 per cent. Moreover, only about one-third of the proposed investment has actually been realised. A study by CMIE showed that private and public investment in industrial projects completed during 1998-2005 amounted to only 1.27 per cent and 0.78 per cent of state GDP, respectively in UP, as against the national average of 1.73 per cent and 1.51 per cent, respectively. Moreover, nearly four-fifth of all completed investments between 2002-2005 went to only three districts—Ghaziabad, Gautam Budh Nagar (both bordering Delhi) and Sonbhadra.

Other indicators of investment flow also reveal a rather bleak picture. For instance, UP's share in bank loans in the country was a paltry 3.30 per cent in 2006. The same was the picture with respect to UP's share in loans from term lending institutions like IDBI, ICICI and REC.

These figures are a clear pointer to the fact that UP is not a favoured destination for investment. A study done for the Twelfth Finance Commission ranked UP at 13th position among major states in terms of the investment attractiveness index (Indicus, 2004).

Constraints on Development

What then, is constraining investment and economic development in the state? Though much can be said and written on this, here we would like to highlight only a few critical factors.

Poor Infrastructure

A major handicap for UP is the low level of infrastructure development which is itself due to the past failures of public policy. In terms of composite index of infrastructural development prepared for the Twelfth Finance Commission, UP stood at the 15th rank among the major states (Mohanty, 2004).

Power is the most critical bottleneck the state is currently facing. There has been practically no addition to generation capacity in the state since 1990, while the demand has been increasing. The distribution network is obsolete and overloaded, resulting in frequent breakdowns. All major cities and towns of the state face power cuts of 4 to 6 hours daily. The T&D losses are extremely high at around 40 per cent, with widespread and open power theft. Consequently, the state power utilities are incurring huge financial losses and have no resources to invest in power generation and for improving the distribution network.

Road density is much lower than in the developed states. The maintenance of roads is poor, adding to the transport cost and time. A major shortcoming is the poor linkage with the rural areas. Nearly 40 per cent of the villages are not connected to all-weather roads. This is a major factor in weak linkages between the urban and the rural areas.

UP is deficient in rural infrastructure in terms of banking, warehousing, cold storages, roads, etc. The public irrigation system is in a bad shape, unable to recover even the operational cost. Area irrigated by canals and public tubewells has been shrinking. The cooperative credit structure in the state has almost collapsed.

The major cities of the state are suffering from the problem of poor urban infrastructure. Urban services like power and water supply are in an abysmal condition and is under increasing pressure due to continuous migration from rural areas. Problems of congestion and pollution are acute. Few cities can boast of an effective infrastructure to attract investment. The financial position of the urban bodies is poor, causing under investment in urban infrastructure.

Distortionary Policy and Regulatory Regime

The policy framework in the state is not conducive for promoting investment and economic growth. Rigidities in land, labour and product markets are a constraint on investment and restrict economic activity. A few examples may be given here:

(i) The land market is not active. There are restrictions on conversion of agricultural land to non-agricultural land. The non-SCs are prohibited from purchasing land owned by SCs. Land leasing is banned by law, though oral leases prevail in practice.

(ii) UP has also been reluctant to bring about changes in the Agricultural Produce and Marketing Act. This prohibits entry of other agencies in agricultural produce markets. A number of other acts put restrictions on procurement, processing and marketing of agricultural produce. All these regulations have been retarding the growth of agro-processing industry, an area in which UP has considerable advantage. The most glaring case is that of sugar industry which is subject to price control on both cane and sugar.

(iii) The burden of regulatory mechanism and restrictive labour laws continues to be relatively heavier in UP and discourages new investments while raising the operating cost of the existing units (Basu, 2006). As many as 6 to 20 clearances have to be obtained to start a new business. Many of the clearances need to be renewed with regular periodicity. Obtaining these clearances is time consuming and cumbersome and creates avenues for 'rent seeking'. The web-enabled system of registration and clearances is not operative in the state unlike in Karnataka and Andhra Pradesh. The industrial units have to comply with a large number of labour laws, which adds to their compliance cost and proves bothersome especially for the small scale units (Singh *et al.,* 2004). Restrictive labour laws including retrenchment and exit liabilities further impose burden on the industry. The minimum wages fixed in UP are higher than the levels prescribed in other states which affects the competitiveness of local industry. Similarly, restriction on contract labour poses a problem to the entrepreneurs to adjust to changing demand conditions in the market.

Over the past decade, the state government has come out with policy declarations on all major sectors of the economy including power, irrigation, transport, tourism, industry, agriculture, etc. These policy declarations are well prepared and attractive documents. However, a large gap remains between policy declaration and its follow up, causing dismay and frustration in the minds of the stakeholders. The other major problem with policy formulation is lack of stability in policy which sends conflicting indicators to the investors. The latest example of the slipshod implementation of policy is the declaration of the new agricultural policy by the present government which was withdrawn within a week of its announcement.

Governance Issues

Good governance is an essential pre-requisite of rapid economic development. UP once was reputed for efficient governance. But there has been a marked decline in the quality of governance over the years (World Bank, 2002; Department of Planning, 2007). Various surveys put UP at the bottom of states in terms of law and order situation, while it is ranked at the top in terms of corruption index. Survey of entrepreneurs put poor law and order situation and corruption, along with poor infrastructure, as the main bottlenecks in industrial growth. Perceptions about corruption and law and order impede the flow of investment into the state (Basu, 2006).

The political instability in the state has, among other things, led to decline in the quality of governance. One dimension of this decline is the growing nexus between the political masters and some sections of the bureaucrats. The threat of frequent transfers and suspensions has demoralised the bureaucracy and undermined its initiative to take policy decisions in an objective, impartial manner. The short tenures have adversely affected the efficiency of the civil servants.

The process of economic reforms in the state is slow and halting. The continuation of controls and regulations coupled with the lack of transparency encourage the 'rent seeking behaviour' of decision makers. While the government expenditures have increased by leaps and bounds, the systems of monitoring and controls have weakened resulting in widespread leakages of various government programmes and evaluation studies, reports of CAG reveal.

UP is suffering from the virus of institutional decay. The institutions that once enjoyed repute as well-performing organisations have in most cases become dysfunctional and sick. The quality of public services like education and health has declined due to factors like lack of funds, vacant positions, absenteeism and poor supervision.

The process of decentralisation has been tardy. Three rounds of elections were held for local bodies between 73rd and the 74th Constitutional amendment—in the years 1995, 2001 and 2006—and yet the State cannot boast of effective local self governance. Some progress in financial devolution has taken place but the process of the transfer of functions and functionaries to the local bodies has been lacklustre. Very few functions have been transferred to the PRIs. The primary education and health care system has not been brought under the control of the PRIs, nor has a separate cadre of local bodies been created. The urban local bodies remain under effective control of the state government. The effort towards empowerment and capacity building of the local bodies have remained weak and halting. The PRIs are functioning basically as the agencies of the government to implement schemes and programmes devised from above, rather than acting as genuine institutions of local self government, as envisaged in the Constitution. They have yet to be genuinely empowered.

Absence of Development-Oriented Leadership

Quality leadership at the top has been the critical factor in all the states which have shown dynamism and faster growth. Uttar Pradesh has suffered for the lack of a development-oriented and dynamic leadership with a few exceptions. During the four decades after Independence when the Congress Party was in power, the state leadership remained dwarfed by the national level leadership. It was only Narain Dutt Tewari who had a developmental vision for the state. It was during his four tenures as Chief Minister that there was a distinct improvement in the investment levels, reflected in the faster economic growth witnessed between 1975-1990.

During the last two decades, the state has been passing through a process of political and social churning resulting in communal strifes, social tensions and political instability. Political mobilisation has also been along caste and communal lines rather than on economic and social issues leading to the emergence of parties like BJP, SP and BSP (Pai, 2007). Grabbing power and using it for personal gain has become a common practice for politicians. Under these circumstance developmental issues have taken a back seat.

Finally, we would like to stress the weak role of the civil society in the state. The intelligentsia, drawn mainly from the upper caste has not shown the kind of concern for the social and developmental issues which is expected of them. It has little sympathy for the teeming millions of the downtrodden, illiterate and poor masses belonging to the backward and scheduled castes. The academia has also not raised the issue of social problems and lack of development in the state in a forceful manner. The NGOs and civil society movement have been relatively weak, though there have been some positive developments in this direction in the recent years.

The Road Ahead

Uttar Pradesh is faced with the daunting challenge of speeding up its development to keep pace with the high rate of growth in the rest of the nation and to deal with the problems of poverty, illiteracy and poor health of the people. Development has, therefore, made the central agenda of the government, the political parties, the intelligentsia and the civil society at large. The two positive developments, which raise hope in this respect are, first, the formation of a popular government with a clear mandate, promising political stability in the state and second, the improvement in the government's fiscal situation, widening the leeway for raising public investment. But much would depend upon how much priority the top leadership gives to the developmental issues and creating an investment-friendly climate. If it fails to do so, the great opportunity thrown up by a stable government and the fiscal ray of hope would be lost.

As our analysis has indicated, to push up the rate of growth of the state economy, investment levels have to be substantially augmented. While the need of public investment in required economic and social infrastructure is indubitable, the bulk of investment has to come through the private sector. Hence, the first priority should be to create a suitable investment climate and industrial bottlenecks removed.

Removing the infrastructure gap deserves the highest priority. The most critical requirement at present is the improvement in the power situation, without which one cannot expect high industrial and agricultural growth. Improvement in road network and better connectivity to villages are needed to unleash the growth potential of the state, particularly in the rural areas. The initiatives that the present state government has taken to promote investment in infrastructure through public-private participation are a welcome step.

Equally important is to step up an attractive and conducive policy environment to attract investment. The distortionary economic policies affecting the working of the land, labour and product market have to be set right to make UP industry competitive. The process of economic reforms and deregulation has to be speeded up. Procedures have to be streamlined and simplified and regulatory burden eased. System of automatic and time bound clearances through web-enabled systems has to be put in place as some other states have done. Discretionary controls have to be minimised to reduce opportunities for 'rent seeking'.

Wide ranging governance reforms have to be undertaken with a view to improve the law and order situation, minimise corruption, improve the functioning of government organisations. Transparency, accountability and responsiveness of administration are the hallmark of good governance. The management of critical infrastructure like power, roads and irrigation has to be professionalised. The excessive state control on the organisations has to be eased and operational autonomy has to be provided to the organisations within the set parameters by the state, so that they are able to take decisions based on economic rather than political considerations. The quality of public services delivery has to be improved at the cutting edge level. The issues of shortage of staff and their training have to be addressed on a priority basis.

The process of decentralisation has to be speeded up by empowering the local bodies and transferring the functions earmarked for them in the Constitution, along with funds and functionaries to discharge their constitutional responsibility. Measures for capacity building of the local bodies have to be carried out in right earnest. Only an empowered decentralised polity would be able to bring administration closer to the people, improve the functioning of the grass roots level institutions and make them responsive to peoples' needs.

Finally, I would like to underline the need for streamlining the policy-making system in the state. At present policy-making is disjointed with nobody to take a comprehensive and long-term view of things. The State Planning Commission, which is lying in a moribund state, should be reorganised to perform this function. It should consist of eminent public figures and experts who should be whole-time members backed by a technically competent secretariat. Only then can it work as a think tank for the development of the state.

The reform agenda proposed above is indeed a tall order and would require visionary leadership and determined efforts. The leadership and the people of the state have to rise to take up this challenge if UP has to come out of its present political, social and economic morass rather than continue to be labelled as the eternally sick state of the country, pulling down the country's progress.

References

Basu, Priya (2006). *Unleashing the Industrial Growth Potential of Uttar Pradesh*. New Delhi: World Bank.

Department of Planning (2007). *Uttar Pradesh Human Development Report 2003*. Lucknow: Government of U.P.

Indicus (2004). *Measuring Inter-State Differences in Investment Attractiveness*. Report Prepared for Twelfth Finance Commission. New Delhi.

Mohanty (2004). *State Infrastructure Index*. Report Prepared for Twelfth Finance Commission. New Delhi.

Pai, Sudha (ed.) (2007). *Political Process in Uttar Pradesh: Identity, Economic Reforms and Governance*. New Delhi: Pearson Longman.

Singh, Ajit Kumar (2000). "Uttar Pradesh economy under the Plans: Low growth and structural stagnation", *Man and Development*. Chandigarh.

———. (2001). *Uttar Pradesh Development Report 2000*. Lucknow: New Royal Book Co.

———. (2007). "The economy of Uttar Pradesh since the 1990s: Economic stagnation and fiscal crisis," in Pai, Sudha (ed.), *Political Process in Uttar Pradesh: Identity, Economic Reforms and Governance*. New Delhi: Pearson Longman.

World Bank (2002). *Poverty in India: The Challenge of Uttar Pradesh*. Washington D.C: Poverty Reduction and Economic Management Sector Unit.

6 Development of Uttar Pradesh

Performance and Prospects

V. Ravi Shankar

In the 1990s, when the rest of India's development work accelerated, Uttar Pradesh slowed down. This slowdown ended with a fiscal crisis in the state at the end of the decade. The fiscal performance has been more responsible since 2000 but there is still a big risk that the power sector losses may result in another crisis. Agriculture has performed relatively well in recent years, as compared to other sectors within the state and to agriculture in the rest of India. Poor infrastructure and red tape are the main constraints to the growth of the private sector, especially small and medium enterprises. Fiscal reforms have expanded budget space but translating outlays to outcomes is a big challenge. Lack of accountability and the weak voice of people's protests are among the reasons for the low quality services and programmes for the poor.

Recent trends, however, have shown that rural areas have seen greater poverty reduction. Much of this comparison is based on National Sample Survey. The UP Government has been doing an additional module on poverty social monitoring indicators, comparing 1994 and 2005. Self-employed farmers experienced the greatest movement out of poverty. Agricultural wages have risen as labour shifted to non-farm activities, both in rural as well as urban areas. The latest report that the World Bank is working on also analyses the situation in four regions, the central, southern, western and eastern UP. There is a very significant decline in rate of poverty in the southern region, where the quantum of irrigated land has increased significantly enough to catch up with the central region of the state. Poverty rates have gone down by 29 percentage points in south UP and by 18 percentage points in central UP but the performance has generally been poor in west and east UP.

Fiscal progress seems to be an important priority with the BSP Government. The aggregate fiscal situation has improved since 2000 and 2006-2007 and has actually recorded a surplus. The new government's decision to introduce value added tax (VAT) is significant because previous governments had hesitated on this count. The previous regimes didn't have the political will to deal with the traders but the present regime has managed to handle them adeptly, having learned from other states. The government has shown that it is willing to take on technical help for this and have put their best officers in charge. This is certainly a positive development which should positively impact the investment climate as well. But most importantly, the government needs to address its unfinished agenda, such as reducing power sector losses and moving from outlays to outcomes.

As observed by Prof. Ashutosh Varshney, a political scientist who has done significant studies on Uttar Pradesh, the BSP's politics of dignity—meaning assertion of Dalit dignity—is being developed in such a manner as to get a more stable political majority and it does mean that development is a priority on the party's agenda. The Chief Minister has been emphasising on improving the law and order situation and this, according to Prof. Varshney, would help in advancing the political and developmental agenda. It will help the BSP's political agenda because the BSP's vote base constituencies comprise those that are the victims of goondaism and atrocities and it will facilitate the economic agenda because improved law and order is vital to industrial and economic development.

Next to law and order is employment. The government has shown the intent to create jobs and has actively expressed itself against giving doles to the unemployed. All these urgent issues call for result-oriented discussions among government officials and experts. Its decision to clean up the public procurement system and for involving PPPs, both in infrastructure as well as in social services are the other positive aspects of the present regime. In terms of infrastructure, projects such as the big expressways cutting across the state—the Taj Expressway and the Ganga Expressway—as well as new airport in greater Noida are major and bold initiatives.

While it is addressing the need to industrialise the western region, the state government seems to have reached a financial closure on investing in the much-needed power projects and are going in for these huge roads and expressways. There is also an overall regulatory simplification. The eastern region will need diversification, higher returns from agriculture both in terms of increase in productivity as well as in terms of improved market access. This would indeed improve the economic returns for the farmers.

There are clear indications that the private sector is satisfied with the measures taken by the present government. In fact, there are indications that the private sector would want to be involved not only in the implementation but also in the consultation stage in the planning of big initiatives. The private sector has gone beyond the stage of merely demanding incentives, sops or making complaints. There is need for a systematic approach to develop a business regulatory reform. Such reforms have been carried out in the past through a single window, single table mechanism but now a much more comprehensive system needs to be put in place to reduce business costs.This PPP framework needs to be very transparent and needs to be mainstreamed because its scope is vast, that is, it goes even beyond the mega projects outlined by the government.

The World Bank has prepared a study of agricultural marketing in UP. The study found the farmers are not happy with the present system of near-total state monopoly, as it limits access to the markets in most regions barring western UP. The farmers fear the unknown, which in this case translates in to the apprehension that the corporations would loot them. This is an area where some analytical work needs to be done on the costs and benefits of changing this system by opening it up to private enterprise to build markets. The ensuing public debate would help formulate the right policy.

Transparency is another focus area and ever since the government computerised their treasury mechanism, there has been a big increase in the disclosure of financial information on the website. But there is, of course, scope for improvement. Transparency in public procurement process is an area that the government could work on, as also on displaying programme budgets and beneficiary lists in villages.

Effective governance, accountability and stability of tenure are essential for delivering results in development. The government needs to rationalise transfer of officers and publish aggregate data regularly, which is not a very difficult task. The Civil Services Board has been reactivated and some order has been brought into everything below the top IAS rung. Change in business processes has to be carried out as envisaged under VAT which would greatly help check corruption.

One of the foremost tasks for the government is to slash down losses in the power sector. Investments may have started to flow in for increasing the generating capacity, but its distribution is the trouble area. One way out would be for the government to choose a few towns for aggressive loss reduction and showcase them.

There were several years when the accounts were not even audited, though, thankfully the new regime is doing something about it. UP's urban population is less than the average for India but the pace of population influx is faster than the national average. Half the towns in UP do not have sewerage, over 33 per cent are without safe drinking water and there are only seven big corporations that qualify for the Jawaharlal Nehru Mission. If urban reforms measures are not speedily scaled up, majority of its citizen will further be bereft of basic amenities. Finally, the intellectual capital of the state has to be galvanised. This would involve tapping institutions like IIT Kanpur and IIM Lucknow. The new, stable government is indeed a window of opportunity. There are several ongoing World Bank projects and some new ones in the pipeline. We are in a preparatory mode for another development policy operation and we hope better ideas will flow to and from the government.

7 Quality Employment in Uttar Pradesh

Scenario and Strategies

Ravi Srivastava

During the span of the 11th Five Year Plan, the labour force in India will grow roughly by about 55 million. Keeping in mind the backlog, we will have roughly about 80 million persons who will be unemployed at the end of the 11th Plan. An overwhelming proportion of these people will be doing some work or the other in the unorganised sector. The Planning Commission has actually emphasised and the National Commission for Enterprises in the Unorganised Sector (NCEUS) has re-emphasised that in this context, we have to focus on growth of productivity and earnings in the unorganised sector. The basic issue which we have talked about and accepted widely—including by the Planning Commission—is that one has to emphasise not only on the quantitative dimensions of employment but actually about generating quality employment. In other words, employment which gives higher remuneration, as also provides better working conditions. It is in this context that one needs to discuss the employment situation in UP.

The quantum and composition of growth in UP is really a matter of concern. It has indeed been a downhill journey from 1950-51, when UP's per capita income was close to the national average. By 2006-07, it had slipped down to 42 per cent of the national average. During the 6th and 7th Plan period, there was a bit of catching up but since 1992-93 the gap between India's average and UP has widened very rapidly. In the last three or four years, when India has been growing at close to 9 per cent, UP has grown at less than two-thirds of that figure, at around 5.5 per cent.

The structure of the state's growth is much more agriculture-oriented, although the tertiary sector is growing at a faster rate than the rest of the country. Clearly, the state has experienced a slower rate of diversification than the all-India economy. But the performance of all the sectors is a matter of concern. The sharpest deceleration has taken place in the last 15 years in the industrial sector. One also needs to make the point rather sharply that about 20 years ago, UP was already in the bottom pile, but atleast it was at the top of this bottom pile of states which included UP, Bihar, Madhya Pradesh, Rajasthan, Orissa and Assam. Now, UP is just above the bottom most of the heap, with Madhya Pradesh, Rajasthan and Orissa having outperformed it in very significant ways.

But analysis has established that in India, being a poor state does not mean having a higher rate of unemployment. The reason is that the poor take up any work, however low in pay and quality, just to survive. This is true for UP too. It is a low income state with low unemployment rates, whether you look at the overall unemployment rate, the youth unemployment rate or the educated unemployment rate. So, the issue is not really so much of unemployment but the quality of employment. UP's employment is concentrated in low productivity sector. The state has a much higher proportion of informal sector employment—the word is used in the way the Commission has now defined and quantified it, which is different from the way the Government of India has traditionally looked at it—and this amounts to about 92.5 per cent, which is considerably higher than the national average, which is at 86.3 per cent. A much larger proportion of the state's workforce is in agriculture and this amounts to 59.8 per cent. Significantly, this entire force is in the unorganised sector. Even more significantly, unorganised sector or the informal sector has the largest numbers, even in the manufacturing and non-agricultural sectors. In the manufacturing sector 81.4 per cent comes from the unorganised segment whereas the national average is 71.6 per cent. In manufacturing, 15.9 per cent are in the unorganised sector, the national average being 13.2 per cent.

Simply put, employment is concentrated in the low productivity sectors. In fact, all direct indicators also point to poor quality employment and more informal work and here, we have made a distinction between informal employment and informal sector. Ninety-six per cent of workers in UP are informally employed, as opposed to the national estimate of 92.4 per cent. There is a much smaller number of workers in the organised sector per thousand population. Only 10 per cent of workers are regular workers as compared to the national average of 15 per cent and this is the result of the way the labour market functions—lower wages and a higher percentage of workers with wages below the national minimum. The persistent picture you get is concentration of employment in low productivity sector in the informal sector with low returns and hence, the fact that large proportion of people in the state stay poor.

The structural characteristics of the workforce also show backwardness. Educational attainment is as low as 14.5 per cent of the population, which is lower than the all-India rate, whether one looks at the workforce or total population, with a middle school level of attainment. If quality is factored in, then the differential with the national average would be much larger. But first, there has to be a more focused discussion on the issue of quality. UP has a very low quality of education—lower than the average for formal skills which itself has only 8.5 per cent workers in the age group 15 to 29 with any skills, compared to about 12 per cent nationwide. And only 1.8 per cent of workers in UP have any formal skills, as compared to the national level of 4 per cent. There are all other kinds of disparities including gender and class/caste disparities.

The question of social security and safety net programmes for the poor have implications for quality of life and employment and they also determine the employment characteristics. An analysis of all major safety net programmes in India, including the National Rural Employment Guarantee Programme (NREGP), along with state-wise comparison of performance has shown that in almost all major programmes the consistently lowest performance was in three states: Bihar, Jharkhand and UP.

What kind of an employment strategy does a state like UP need? Firstly, the focus has to be on the demand and supply issues. It has to be based on a strategy in which high productivity sectors get high investments and are in the driver's seat. But one must realise that the high productivity sectors in UP or India do not generate direct employment, they have huge indirect spin-offs and linkages in terms of technology, including backward and forward linkages. In this context, sunrise sectors like manufacturing and services as also multi-sectors like cultural tourism—which has a huge scope in a state like UP—have to be identified. But a major emphasis has to be to promote growth and productivity in low productivity sectors, such as agriculture and the informal sector.

The informal sector is of great importance in UP. Both the national and the state scenario suggest that the unorganised non-agriculture sector would absorb the bulk of the incremental labour force and hence its role is crucial. On the supply side, I have already emphasised the role of education and skills and of course the role of effective social security net programmes. So basically, you need a very broad-based strategy which can focus on all these elements with a special emphasis on the role of the unorganised sector.

In UP, 92 per cent of enterprises are smaller, weaker and gets less support than it does in the rest of the country. Even if you look at manufacturing with its huge returns, about 42 per cent of it comes from unregistered manufacturing and if that number was added on, the percentage would be much larger. But if you analyse it, 92 per cent of the enterprises are owner-count units, only 7 per cent employ 2-5 workers and only 1 per cent employs 6 to 9 workers. This also implies that there are much smaller assets for an enterprise, much smaller gross value added per worker and much smaller gross value added per enterprise. It must also be noted that only 2 per cent of such enterprises in UP get any credit from institutional sources as compared to 4 per cent nationally. It all paints a very poor picture of the kind of profile and support that you have for this entire sector in UP.

Household manufacturing is a crucial component of industry in UP. Up to the 90s, household manufacturing was declining in UP as it was in the whole nation but between 1991-2001, there has been a spurt in the segment. Employment in this area has grown at three times the rate than non-household manufacturing. A lot of it is sub-contracting and has to do with specific sectors, but there can be little doubt that in UP's context, one needs to recognise there is a very specific niche in traditional unorganised industry. UP has the largest percentage of workers in traditional industries, such as textiles and handloom but it has not been able to put together a proactive policy environment to accelerate the growth of this sector and enhance the incomes of those employed in it.

The major problems in terms of overall industrial growth can be listed as follows: one, lack of consistent policy. No industrial policy regime has lasted for more than three to five years; two, poor implementation in governance. Most of the policies remain only on paper; three, poor infrastructure and poor power supply; four, poor law and order situation. All these four areas have to be addressed and one needs to proactively support employment-friendly growth. This basically means facilitating the increase in the number of producers in all sectors, keeping in view the changing facets of the new economic environment.

One of the characteristics of the new, globalisation oriented-economic environment is increased competitiveness among enterprises. There is political competition in every state in the country but many states, such as Tamil Nadu have more or less evolved a common economic agenda, putting aside political rivalry. If at all there is competition in this sphere, it is in terms of competitive economic populism. But in UP, any such common economic agenda is conspicuous by its absence. This is something that people who are in politics and economics needs to reflect on in order to develop a new economic, industrial and employment strategy.

8 The Sick Public Health System in Uttar Pradesh

The Malaise and Prescriptions

Santosh Mehrotra

While writing the chapter on poverty reduction for the 11th Five Year Plan, I noted an interesting fact related to the incidence and concentration of poverty. In 1993-94, four states accounted for 49 per cent of the poor of the country. These were Uttar Pradesh, Bihar, Maharashtra and Madhya Pradesh. The point to be noted is that the geographic concentration of poverty has increased in the last 10 years with economic growth. In other words, we have a situation where these four states—two of them split in to Jharkhand and Chhattisgarh—now account for 58 per cent of the poor of the country. So the geographic concentration of poverty in the country is actually increasing and UP is contributing to that.

There is a very direct link between health system and poverty outcomes. UP has one of the lowest per capita public health expenditure and as a result private health expenditure is high. Private health expenditure as a proportion of total health expenditure is at 92 per cent, way above the national average of 79 per cent. High private health expenditure is not only inequitable, as it adversely impacts the poorest people in one of the poorest states in India but is also highly inefficient. Per capita expenditure on health in Uttar Pradesh is Rs. 84. It is far below the average of all the states in India, which stands at Rs. 207. Private health expenditure is one of the most important causes for families going below the poverty line. According to NSS surveys of 1973-74 and 2004-05, UP is one of the six states in the country where the number of poor has not declined for over 30 years. The argument that follows from an assessment of this situation is that there has really never been any political commitment to improving the public health delivery system in UP or in the country as a whole. The very fact that only 44 per cent of children in India are fully immunised emphasises this point.

It is a well-known fact that the social outcome indicators of all kinds—health, education, nutrition, etc., in the northern states in India are generally far worse than those prevailing in southern India. A year and a half back, I had written a paper comparing UP with Tamil Nadu and made the specific observations based on data that, despite the fact that we have had governments over the last 15 years which have focused their attention on the lower castes, especially the Dalits and the other backward castes (OBCs), we get very little evidence from outcome indicators that there has been any improvement in the health or nutritional quality of those very castes and classes who were supposed to be the beneficiaries. You will also see a comparison with Bihar and we don't come out looking very well, even though public health infrastructure is actually much better in UP than in Bihar.

The National Rural Health Mission (NRHM), constituted two years ago, carried out a common review of the situation in several states, including UP and it has found the conditions slightly better than it has been over the last 15-20 odd years. But there are still many key prescriptions that needs to be prescribed and the government of UP does not seem to be actually looking at the right medicines. In UP, barely 23 per cent of all children under the age of two have been fully immunised, which is half the Indian average. It is recognised the world over that children are the sapling of health of any community and where they are fully immunised, the public health system functions reasonably well. In many ways, outcome indicators, especially in areas like immunisation is a process indicator. So, only half of the country's children are actually fully immunised—44 per cent, to be exact—and in UP it is about half that figure, that is, 23 per cent. By deduction, it can be said that UP's health system functions at half the effectiveness of India's average.

The data relating to nutritional outcomes present a not-so-inspiring picture all over the country. The Body Mass Index (BMI) of 31 per cent of Indian males and 33 per cent Indian females are below 18.5, which is the cut off for malnutrition. Uttar Pradesh men and women on an average have BMIs lesser than the national average. The national mean BMI for men is 20.2 while it is 19.8 in UP. The national mean BMI for women is 20.5 while it is 20.1 in UP. It can also be seen that while the national average of stunted children under 3 years is 38.4 per cent, in UP it is 46 per cent while it is 42 per cent in Bihar. Percentage of underweight children is 45.9 per cent nationally and 47.3 per cent in UP. Infant mortality rate which determines life expectancy, in a significant sense, is an outcome indicator. We notice that at 73, infant mortality rate in

UP is way above India's 57 and is far worse than Bihar, where it is 62. Again, in terms of the percentage of children who have received all recommended vaccines, the total in UP is 23 per cent but in Bihar it is relatively higher at 33 per cent. So even among the BIMARU states there is a pecking order and increasingly there is evidence that in Madhya Pradesh and Rajasthan, at least the education indicators are moving out of the BIMARU status. In terms of maternal health, only 22 per cent of UP's mothers are delivering babies in health institutions. The rest are all delivering at home. The recommended practice obviously is institutional delivering. Here, UP is not doing any worse than Bihar but is still at half the Indian average. Half of the Indian women had at least three antenatal care visits for their last birth, but the share of UP women is only half of this average. So in many respects UP is doing much worse, not just compared to the nation as a whole, but also even Bihar.

TFR stands for total fertility rate, the number of children a mother of reproductive age between 15 and 49 bears. To reach a stable population, India has to reach a TFR of 2.1. Kerala has 2.1, Tamil Nadu has 2.1, India is at 2.7. UP is way above that at 3.8 and in rural areas of the state, it is as high as 4.1.

In terms of drinking water availability too, UP's statistics are dismal. The percentage of households that use piped drinking water in UP is 10.3 per cent, while the all-India average is 42 per cent. If one compares the figures, 71 per cent of urban India has piped drinking water. It is only 34.8, or half of that in UP. The story is similar *vis-à-vis* access to toilet facility. It is 33 per cent in UP and 44.5 per cent in India.

The abysmally negative statistics above make it abundantly clear that urgent measures are needed to effect a significant fall in infant mortality rates and improvement in nutritional quality. One way of stating this phenomenon is to say that half of India's children are malnourished and half of UP's children are malnourished as well. If this is not found shocking enough, consider this: compared to India's half, only a third of African children are malnourished. In this respect, India, a 'developing' country, is far worse than a typically 'underdeveloped' African country. This brings us to the question: where is UP in terms of health infrastructure? A comparative data is based on the number of people served per government hospital. The national average on this is 1.45 lakh people. In UP it is 1.98 lakh, while in Bihar it is 8.7 lakh. Here one can see that UP's public health infrastructure is actually better than Bihar's. But it has also been recorded that outcome indicators in UP are actually worse despite the fact that the state's infrastructure is slightly better. Population served per government hospital bed is 2,257 in India but 5,646 in UP and 28,959 in Bihar. The average area and the radial distance in square kilometres. from health sub-centres, public health centres (PHC) or from community health centres (CHC) in UP present another revealing picture. These distances are 1.91 radial distance, 4.51 kilometres and 13.9 kilometres respectively, while the corresponding values at the national level are 2.61, 6.3 and 17.22 kilometres, respectively. These figures are not only less than the national average, but are actually similar to the figures prevailing in Kerala. The distance and the area is actually less than the national average and yet UP's outcomes are far worse. In other words, our infrastructure is not that bad. But the one thing that you will hear from the government sources if you go and talk to them would be woes about infrastructure. You would be told that infrastructure is far below the quantum required and what little there is of it is in a mess. I am talking from personal experience, and this apathetic attitude reveals a complete inability to recognise the real problems, not to speak of dealing with them.

However, one of the things that has happened in the last two years is that the country has recognised that we have to give far greater priority to the public health system. A National Rural Health Mission was created two years ago and UP, of course, is one of its priority states. It is evident that the state has benefited a lot. The number of Accredited Social Health Activists (ASHA) and Auxiliary Nursing Midwifes (ANM) has increased considerably, the allocations from the Central government too has increased significantly and there is flexi pool of funds which are available to the various health centres which can be used in different ways. But the big question is about the results. What are the results out of all this? Clearly, UP has a whole history of underfunding and lack of political commitment, but now that the Central government is putting in the money, do we see some changes? The good news is that we are. The NRHM has used about four indicators and assessed the case load being handled by the public system at all levels and has come to the conclusion that there is an actual increase in institutional deliveries. There has been an increase in the availability of drugs. High numbers of out-patients are turning up at public health centres.

One of the specific indicators analysed was in relation to the preparedness of health facilities for in-patient care and utilisation of beds for such care. The conclusion was that while the number of nurses and ANMs have increased, shortage of nursing staff is still a major constraint, the worst being the shortage of specialists. At the same time, the conclusion also has it that the availability of untied funds from the NRHM to the sub-centres has helped in improving the sessions of immunisation and so on. So, things are beginning to look reasonably better but there are whole series of areas which require action. One relates to this long standing issue of appointed doctors not turning up at rural centres. Also, the number of vacant posts is very high. How do we solve this problem? Thankfully, the state government is beginning to think about a scheme that the states of Assam and Chhattisgarh have taken up. This scheme is to start a three years course, instead of expecting doctors who train for five years to go serve for years in rural areas. The other good development is that there is now a Drug Procurement Corporation, somewhat modelled on the lines of Tamil Nadu Government's Corporation. But a lot of action still needs to be taken in order to ensure that doctor-prescription hiccup is cured. This is regarding the habit of PHC doctors prescribing drugs that are not available in the PHC pharmacy. In other words, the patient has to go outside to buy the drugs. There is clear evidence of collusion here between the doctor and the pharmacies outside. Then, there is this issue of performance pay, a long standing issue about whether doctors should be given the freedom to do private practice or not. A via media could be that all doctors who work for government hospitals be first given a base salary and then be paid an added sum, depending on the number of patients they examine, i.e., a performance based add-on. The system would have to be monitored through a biometric card issued to the doctor. But unless there is some marriage of the private incentive to the public pay, I don't think we are going to see much change in the situation.

Medical colleges too are an important segment of the medical infrastructure. One of the things that is repeatedly said about UP is that the state has too few medical colleges compared to southern states and that the Central government should provide assistance for setting them up. We are also told that the UP medical colleges are actually short of staff. So, the answer is to set up more medical colleges, produce more doctors to fully staff the medical colleges. The logic is not entirely flawless because, in point of fact, there are plenty of staff for clinical positions. What they don't get is enough staff for para-clinical and non-clinical positions because there are not enough students who are takers for postgraduate positions. That is the real problem and not the lack of medical colleges or students. In any case, there is the long standing issue of absenteeism. Which means that requisite staff is there but not at their workplace. Also there is a large body of "registered medical practitioners" of highly doubtful credentials practicing—or malpracticing, as the case may be—in the state. The UP Health Department needs to come up with a credible strategy to address this problem, through mechanisms like Lok Sampark Abhiyan.

Even as the steps to address these ground issues are being worked out, there is a need to devise a broad approach. In the first place, the state needs to take conscious and calculated measures to benefit from the increased investment in health during the 11th Five Year Plan. If UP has to increase per capita GDP growth rate, it has to bring down the population growth rate, at least to the national average. TFR must decline to the replacement level of 2.1 but that cannot happen as long as IMR remains well above national average. Hence, top priority must be given to preventive and primary health care services. There is also need for a greater synergy in the training efforts of the National Institute for Health and Family Welfare and the UP State Institute for Health and Family Welfare. Training of rural practitioners should be to promote and actively support public health measures. System-wide needs of infrastructure and human resources need to be made and funds of NRHM utilised for the same.

Figure 8.1

IMR in UP, Bihar and India

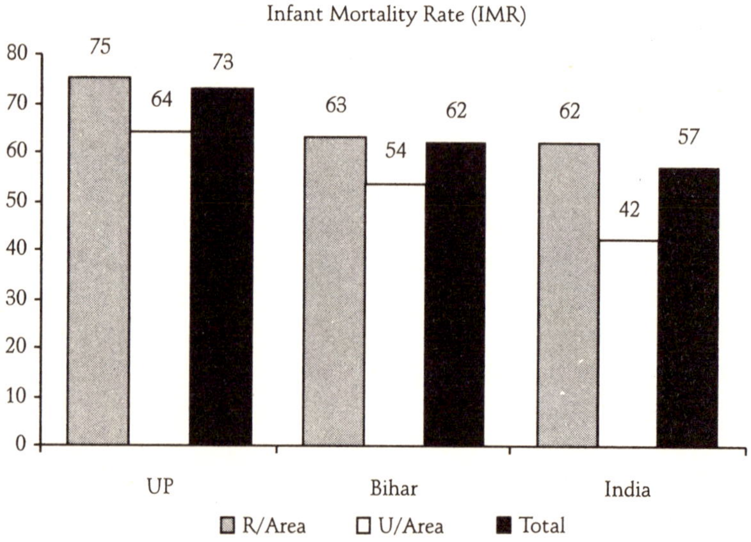

Figure 8.2

Per cent of Children (12-23 months) who have received all Recommended Vaccines

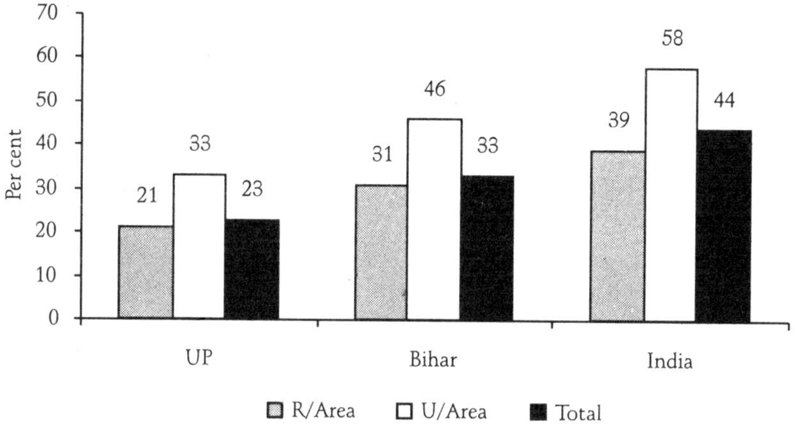

Figure 8.3

Per cent of Mothers who received Supplementary Food and Health Check-ups from AWC while Breastfeeding

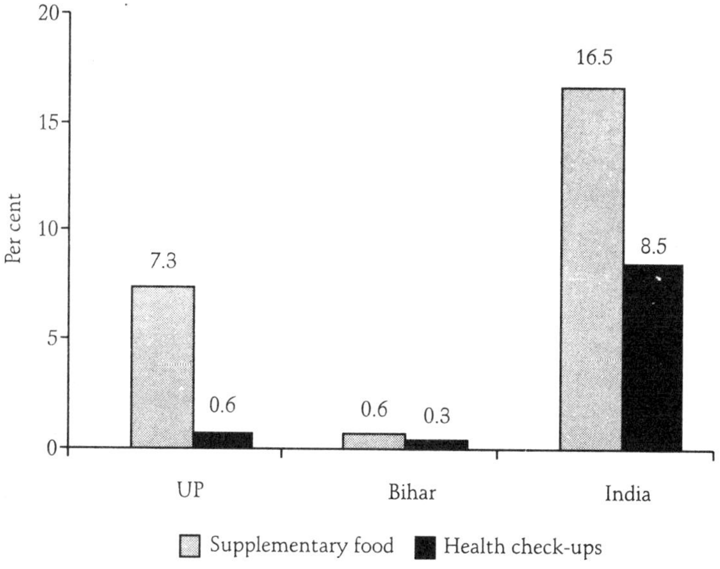

Figure 8.4

Mothers' Antenatal Care Visits (atleast 3) for their Last Birth and Pregnant Women (15-49) who are Anaemic (Per cent)

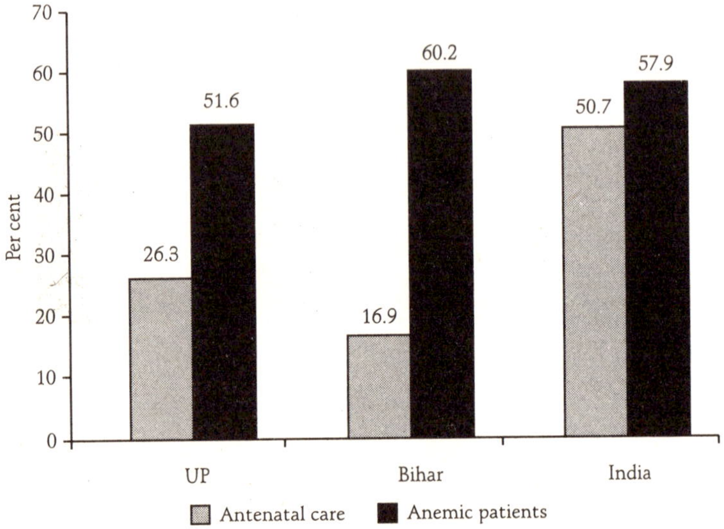

Figure 8.5

Trends in Institutional Deliveries (Per cent)

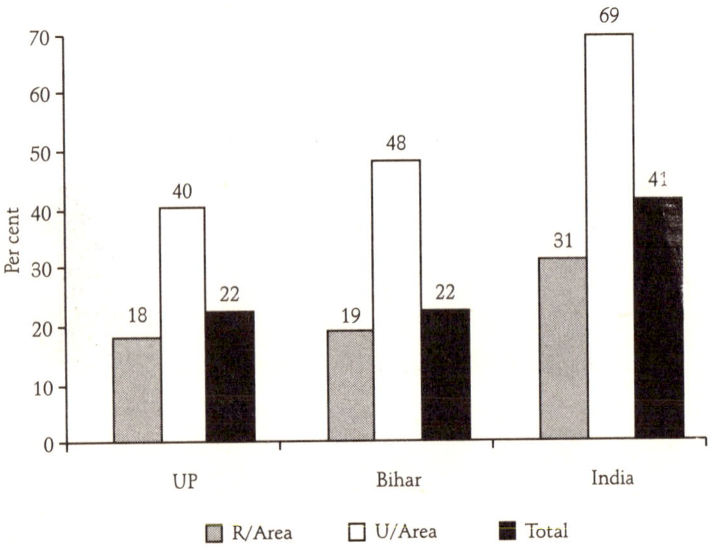

Figure 8.6

TFR in UP, Bihar and India

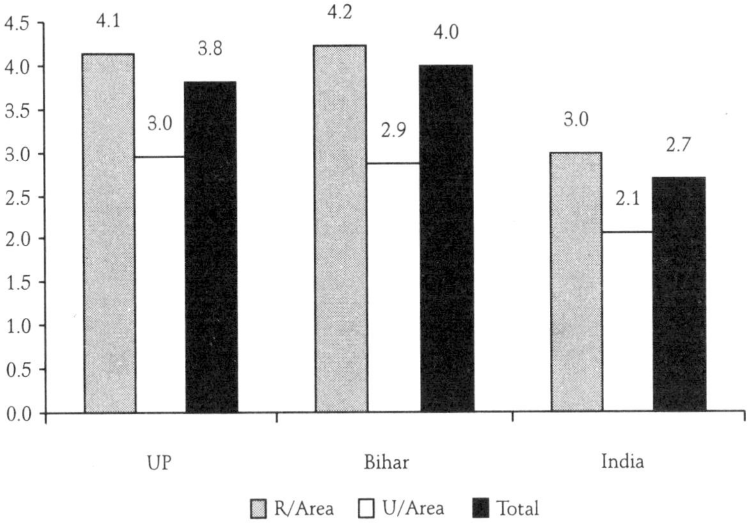

Figure 8.7

Per Capita Expenditure on Health (in Rs.)

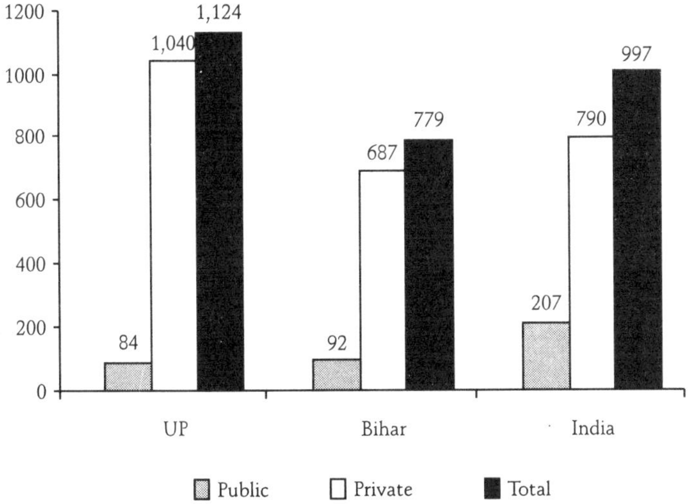

Table 8.1

Nutritional Status (NFHS-III, 2005-06)

Indicators	*UP*	*Bihar*	*India*
Children under 3 years who are			
Stunted (%)	46	42	38.4
Wasted (%)	13.5	28	19.1
Underweight (%)	47.3	58	45.9
Mean BMI for men	19.8	19.9	20.2
Mean BMI for women	20.1	19.4	20.5

Table 8.2

Health Inputs ((NFHS-III, 2005-06)

	Water and Sanitation								
	UP			*Bihar*			*India*		
Indicators	*R/Area*	*U/Area*	*Total*	*R/Area*	*U/Area*	*Total*	*R/Area*	*U/Area*	*Total*
Per cent of HH that use piped drinking water	2	34.8	10.3	1.2	19.8	4.2	27.9	71	42
Per cent of HH that have access to a toilet facility	16	83.7	33.1	16.2	73	25.2	25.9	83.1	44.5

Table 8.3

Status of Operationalisation of AWCs as on 31st March 2007

Particulars	*UP*	*Bihar*	*India*
Total sanctioned (number)	150,727	81,088	1,052,638
Operational (number)	128,859	57,767	844,743
No. of *anganwadi* workers in position	122,341	60,041	814,817
No. of *anganwadi* workers vacant	15,216	20,487	130,988
No. of *anganwadi* helpers in position	120,074	59,797	805,753
No. of *anganwadi* helpers vacant	17,483	20,731	140,052
Children average per *anganwadi*	134	68	77
Mothers average per *anganwadi*	28	14	16

Table 8.4

Public and Private Expenditure on Health, 2001-02

States	Health Expenditure (in Rs.000s)			Public Exp. as a Per cent of Total Expenditure	Private Exp. as a Per cent of Total Expenditure
	Public	Private	Total		
UP	14,088,564	174,025,330	188,113,894	7.5	92.5
Bihar	7,708,790	57,455,419	65,164,209	11.8	88.1
India	214,391,018	818,104,032	1,032,495,050	20.8	79.2

III

Governance and Administration of Uttar Pradesh

9 Towards Overall Stability

Yogendra Narain

Political instability has for long destabilised governance in Uttar Pradesh which, as a consequence, has made a mockery of the bureaucracy and has made it a burden on the shoulder of the public. Since Independence, the state has had 42 chief secretaries, out of whom only three stayed on for more than three years, five lasted a little over two years and most of the rest came and left before they saw the end of a year or so. The state has weathered 38 Chief Ministers, punctuated by three spells of President's rule. Coalition governments have been the order of the day since 1993 and the Chief Ministers—whichever the party—had to make various compromises both on policy as well as administrative issues to stay in power. This has led to a tendency to maximise short term gains rather than address the longer term issues concerning the economic development of the state. Consequently, the secretaries in Lucknow and the officers in the districts have and are being unceremoniously shifted from one position to another after highly truncated tenures, thus habituating them to bow to the powers rather than risk taking independent decisions.

This has played havoc with all public institutions in the state. Asked why officers were not allowed to stay at a post for a decent span of time, a Chief Minister replied: "if Chief Ministers have shorter tenures, why not officers?" With every change of Chief Minister an exodus of officers takes place. The data on these massive transfers is incomplete but between 1992-1998, each Chief Minister has transferred an average of 420 officers per year out of a total cadre of nearly 500 IAS officers not to speak of PCS officers whose transfers are even more. In the early stages after Independence, the tenures of the officers as well as their political masters used to be more durable. The administration therefore, also tended to be strong. However, a recent World Bank study points out that the average tenure is now less than a year and some informal reports put it at less than six months. Over the years, a deluded belief has been growing among political leaders that under the Constitution, it is they who head the administration and therefore, hold the full power to control the administrative set-up. The ethos of rule and administration has been completely changed. Now, ministers are not necessarily appointed because of their abilities but because of the political factions they control. Transfers have become one of the tools that politicians use to make the officers and staff "responsive".

To understand the enormity of the task of governing UP, let us look at some facts and statistics. One-sixth of the world's population are Indians and 1/6th of Indians live in Uttar Pradesh. With 166 million people, it is the most populous Indian state and if it were a country it would be the world's seventh largest country in terms of population. How do we judge the governance of a state like this? Governance of any state can be judged by the following parameters: (i) The actual output in terms of economic and social parameters. (ii) The public perception of governance, which includes the ease with which the ordinary citizen can sort out his problems with the government. UP's output is the second highest in the country, with a net domestic product of Rs. 2,41,196 crore, the highest is Maharashtra with Rs. 3,86,241 crore output. UP continues to be the second largest as far as the State Domestic Product is concerned. In per capita income, though Uttar Pradesh in 2005-06 ranked very low at Rs. 13,262 which is almost half the average for the country, the very next year the rate rose to 11.3 per cent which was very near the national average increase of 12.1 per cent, as given by the economic survey for 2006-2007. Thus, Uttar Pradesh presents a very mixed picture. It has 32.8 per cent people living below the poverty line, which is much higher than the national average of 27.5 per cent. In education, the gross enrolment figure in school for classes 1-5 is 105.74, which almost touches the national average of 107.8. But in classes 6-8 it is less than the national average. The state's literacy rate, as per the 2001 census is 56.27, again much lower than the national average of 64.84 per cent. Health-wise, UP has a very high infant mortality rate of 71, far above the national average of 57. The percentage of households that get safe drinking water is 87.8, about 10 per cent higher than the all-India average of 77.9 per cent. The state's life expectancy is 59.8 years against the all-India average of 63.2. Then again on the low side, the percentage of women giving birth in hospitals and medical institutions is 22 per cent against the all-India average of 40.7 per cent and over 40 per cent children in UP receive no vaccination. The percentage of people having electricity is 42.8 per cent as against the all-India average of 67.9 per cent.

I have tried to trace out the outcomes of governance first and then the public perception. In National Rural Employment Guarantee Act (NREGA), the performance of UP is judged as average or below average in benchmarks like issue of job cards and timely payment of wages and this is as per the citizen's report on governance and development, 2007. However, on the other hand, the employment provided in UP under this programme was 95 per cent of the demand which is very high. The percentage of indebted farmers in Uttar Pradesh is 40.3 per cent which is much lower than the national average of 48.6 per cent. We have no reported farmer suicides which seems to plague advanced and well governed states like Andhra Pradesh, Karnataka, Maharashtra, Punjab and Kerala.

Decentralisation of planning and programmes is necessary to ensure planned regional development, as also the participation and empowerment of the poor. Yet, despite clear directions given through the 73rd and 74th Constitutional Amendments, UP has not moved towards effective decentralisation. No effective transfer of functions, functionaries and finances to local self governments and to the *panchayats*, and no capacity building in institutions like the *gram sabhas* has taken place, with the result that governance at these levels is hit both by poor finances as well as by lack of trained manpower. It has only transferred 12 subjects to local governments as against 29 such transfers in Rajasthan, Tamil Nadu and Haryana. Uttar Pradesh has not even constituted District Planning Committees, while 20 states have already done so, as required under the Constitution.

Another factor by which we can judge governance is transparency and openness. With the enforcement of the Right to Information Act, all government files and decisions have come under public scrutiny. Uttar Pradesh has set up its Information Commission and has also appointed a number of Information Commissioners. However, there have been open complaints about the apathy of the government in providing the required infrastructure to the Information Commission. Thus, there can be little doubt that there has been a negative public perception about governance in Uttar Pradesh for a number of years. In fact the state, which would like to be called 'Uttam Pradesh', is sometimes jokingly called 'Ulta Pradesh'.

Financial administration too reflects the sorry state of affairs. UP's acute fiscal problems have resulted in unsustainable borrowing and the cutting of necessary development expenditure. The state is caught in a vicious circle of low investment, low growth and low revenues leading to further deceleration of development. However, there has been some improvement in the last two or three years in revenue income through sales tax and other receipts. Some of the implications of huge fiscal and revenue deficits are discussed below:

Falling Plan expenditure—Plan expenditure has been falling rapidly since the 5th Plan. This is despite the fact that the devolution from the Government of India both via the Finance Commission and the Planning Commission favours the poorer states, UP being one of them. A wide gap between planned amount and what is actually made available leads to uncertainty in budget releases and corruption. The state has a very low share in the total Plan expenditure. Falling social sector expenditure—that is, in expenditure on education and health as a proportion of total expenditure—can be seen from the fact that in 2000-01, the share for education in the state's total expenditure was 16.8 per cent against India's 17.4 per cent and in 2004-05 it was 12.5 per cent against all India's 13.4 per cent. This shows that the expenditure on social sectors as a proportion of total expenditure has generally been falling over the years and is less than the all-India average. Although there has been improvement in 2004-05 and also in 2005-06, long term trends will be known only when such an increase is sustained in the coming years.

There is no official data on the degree of corruption—the bane of the state, as it is for most states. However, a World Bank survey in 2000 highlighted the all pervasive corruption in the state's lower judiciary, the revenue department, sales tax department and the local bodies. Demand for 'speed money' is the normal practice. In successive surveys of the business community by the journal *Business Today*, administrative corruption and malfeasance was cited as a major deterrent against investment in the state. In 1999, *Business Today* ranked the state as the second worst state to invest in for reason of political instability and poor governance. A survey of the general population around the same time revealed that nearly 57 per cent of the population had to pay bribes to receive public services. Another private survey was carried out in 2005 by the Centre for Media Studies (CMS) which compositely ranked and indexed the states according to the incidence of petty corruption in deals between the common citizen and 11 public service organisations. The composite index of Uttar Pradesh was 491 and it ranked 10th in the country, again in the middle—not at the top in corruption, but certainly not without a heavy dose of it. Generally, areas that deal with electricity, schools and income tax figure high in the corruption raging in Uttar Pradesh, as reported by CMS. The Government of Uttar Pradesh in 2000 had taken note of this and together with the World Bank formulated a strategy to restore the efficiency and integrity of the civil services. The state did try to develop a viable anti-corruption strategy and strengthen accountability institutions like the Lok Ayukt and the vigilance establishments. It formed citizen's charters to improve service delivery. The results, in the long run, were mixed. The backlog of vigilance and Lok Ayukt reports were cleared and the number of investigations increased but another political transition took place after a few months and again the emphasis on these measures was reduced. Uttar Pradesh demonstrates the limits of reforms. All too often the requirements of sound administration has come up against and has been overwhelmed by the state's social fragmentation and the politics of power grabbing.

The National Crime Records Bureau for the period between 1999 and 2006 reveals that the incidents of total cognisable crimes under the IPC in UP ranges between 130,000 to 127,000 every year. But if you take the number of crimes commited per lakh population, the rate comes down. So you can argue all you want about whether the glass is half full or half empty but it will not change the fact that crime rages in the state. But all this analysis is on the basis of registered cases. One hears the complaint repeatedly, even from top leaders, that a large number of crimes go unregistered. The police complain that its budget is so low that there have been cases where people who go to the *thanas* (police stations) for registration and investigation have been asked to pay for the petrol expenses of the jeep or buy stationery, which is always in short supply. Uttar Pradesh spends around Rs.2,500 crore on its police force, but only 33 per cent of the officers are provided housing. The police is a very dissatisfied and defeated lot indeed. Large sums of money exchange hands during police recruitment and even officers of DIG level have been suspended for such actions. All the same, one positive point has been that there are less communal incidents in the state.

Caste-based politics has dominated both governance and administration, playing a major role in postings. But then, this is a common feature in many states, even in the well-administered ones like Tamil Nadu, Karnataka and Andhra Pradesh. In the initial post-Independence era, it used to be a tussle between the Brahmins, the Vaishyas, the Kayasthas or the Thakurs but now it is between the scheduled castes, political groups and the OBC groups. In the earlier years the posting of officers was not based on caste considerations but now it is increasingly so in UP, specially in the last decade. We also see a unique political phenomenon these days. If a particular scheme is sanctioned by one political party in power, it is completely nullified and demolished by the opposing political party which comes into power in the next election. This is a huge waste of public money. However, in a democracy, there is no way it can be prevented, since the elected party has the mandate of the people.

Where does Uttar Pradesh's governance go from here? The state government faces the challenge of maintaining the quality of governance in the state, increasing accountability and reducing the incidences of administrative misconduct leading to corruption. However, any strategy to improve the quality of governance will need to have three components. First, a redefinition of the role of the government, specifically a reduction of its role in the economy through deregulation and disinvestments, so that it is able to focus its limited capacity in those areas in which it has comparative advantages. Second, a programme of civil service renewal is required, so that the government can better perform its core functions. Third, significant gains in service quality and accountability by efficiently planning the devolution of spending responsibilities and revenue raising powers to elected local bodies. In the areas of civil service reform, the government continues to face three critical challenges. It must first enhance the productivity of the civil services and ensure that every employee is performing a socially relevant task. Secondly, it must create procedures for awarding merit and for punishing malfeasance and misconduct, thus enforcing accountability and improving performance. Thirdly, the cutting edge level of the bureaucracy needs to be adequately trained and professionalised.

The BSP Government, in power with a majority since the the 2007 May elections, has the potential to embark on this course. This opportunity of a single party majority has come after a long time and how this regime moves forward is crucial for the state's progress. The civil services will also have to play their due role creatively, fully enabling the use by the public of legislations such as the Right to Information Act. A strong culture must develop in the services to resist wrongdoing by convincing the political leaders. Whistle blowing must be encouraged and the citizens/NGOs should be motivated to file PILs in cases where the administration is being pressurised to commit acts of illegality. Last but not the least, the civil servants must not themselves be intimidated to do wrong under peer pressure. The IAS association should continue with the internal voting mechanism to identify the most corrupt officers and put officers under suspicion on the watch list, as an additional peer measure.

What have been listed in this chapter are essentially the broad parameters of how governance has existed in the state for the past decade or so and some pointers for effecting a course correction. Admittedly, it is easy to list out things on paper and very difficult to implement them on the ground. The state government, the bureaucracy and indeed the people of UP has a long tough distance to cover before it regains its glory of the pre-Independence days.

10 Governance and Administration

Accountability is the Issue

Prakash Singh

During one of my visits to Chhattisgarh, I was appalled to be told that a large, remote area known as Abujmar, covering 4000 sq km did not exist on the revenue map of India, nor was there any police presence. No land survey had ever been carried out and in short, there was absolutely no administrative presence. The area was an open invitation for Naxalites to come and take over, which they promptly did. Today, it is their stronghold from where they launch their activities.

Since a few years after Independence, governance in UP began to degenerate into an instrument in the hands of various groups of political (self) interests that cared little about the welfare of the state and its people. It has now reached such a point that it has wrested, from Bihar, the position of being the worst ruled state in India. (In the last year or two, Bihar's efficiency graph has been showing, however slowly, a steadily rising trend.) UP's problems are no different from many of the other states—poverty, illiteracy, poor infrastructure and worst of all, an abysmal power situation. What is different is that the problems are more intense than in any other state and as certain denominators indicate, its figures are comparable to Sub-Saharan Africa. All this is a pathetic commentary on the administration of UP.

The paradox is that the state has a brilliant array of officers, be it of the IAS or IPS and yet it is at the bottom rung of the ladder. The national parties, the Congress and the Bharatiya Janata Party in the state have been marginalised and have hardly any chance of making a comeback. It is now a ding-dong battle between the regional forces, the ruling Bahujan Samaj Party and the Samaj Party. Sadly, these parties are bereft of both vision and earnest intent except, when in power, to feather their nest. Regardless of who is in power, caste rules the roost. If one party projects one caste or castes, the other party, as soon as it comes to power, 're-castes'—if one may coin a word—the whole scenario. Whether for a posting in the secretariat or in key positions elsewhere, an officer is chosen on caste and loyalty credentials and not on his merit. What is worse, with an incomprehensibly immature sense of vengeance, if one government takes up a positive plan or project, the next government will either drop or delay the project just out of spite.

Corruption, the partner in arms to casteism, is rampant, as we all know. There is an organisation called India Rejuvenation Initiative, of which I am a member. We decided to identify the most corrupt officers of the state, not only in UP but all over the country. We started with UP because we had more inputs from UP than from other states and prepared a list of the most corrupt IAS and IPS officers. We are focusing on these two because if these two are set right, the rest will follow. We sent the list to the higher authorities and that is that. Nothing has moved. In 2006, I sent their names to the Union Minister and was really hopeful that something would move. All he had to do was to write to Chairman, CBDT, to initiate inquiries into their assets. After four months I reminded the Secretary and I got a cryptic response, to the effect that the minister had seen the letter. That is the end of the matter. I have started to have serious doubts that the governments, Central or state, consider corruption as a serious issue, whether even the best of the ministers have the guts to tackle corruption.

I even wrote a letter against five odd judges of the Lucknow High Court to the State Chief Justice, informing him that they were all corrupt. But the Chief Justice is, as yet, sleeping over it. Two of these were rewarded by the political establishment with higher positions after retirement and one of them is today a Chief Justice in one of the High Courts. What it simply comes to is this: Raise your voice against corruption and the entire establishment—State and Central—goes in to a *mauna dharma* (vow of silence). The entire machinery of governance is too 'well-oiled' to produce even a squeak.

It is said the officer has the right to freedom of speech. Indeed he does, but does any of them have the courage to speak out? How can you inject courage into somebody? Certain officers start working on gubernatorial assignments towards the fag end of their careers and start compromising their position. Is there remedy for all this? There is a remedy and that remedy is institutional. One has to build institutional mechanisms that insulate officers from political pressures and influences. This had been my effort when I went to the Supreme Court for reforms in the police. When I proposed the setting up of a state security commission, an establishment board and a complaints authority, the idea was to raise institutions that would enable an officer, even under most adverse circumstances, to speak out and to assert himself. Admitted, there is a limit to how far you can go. But certain institutional mechanisms and institutional safeguards can be operative once you are given a fixed tenure of two years.

Also, no voice is raised over the huge, unaccounted waste of public money. What I found deeply distressful in Lucknow is that people are just not prepared to speak against the establishment. If you take up an issue and say that you want to go to the High Court or move an application, nobody is prepared to sign the document. As for the police, despite all their claims to the contrary, their performance in keeping peace and order has been abominable. In a comparative study, a UP police document claims that there has been a sharp decline of 20 per cent in murders, 31.7 per cent in dacoity, 38.4 per cent in loot, 21.3 per cent in riots and 8.3 per cent in burglary. This only means that thousands of cases have gone unregistered. There was a similar report during the reign of another government. It claimed 70 per cent reduction in crime. Did the new government gift the police with a magic wand? No one accepted or challenged it. The prevailing and depressing sentiment is: "What is the point?"

I took up the matter with the National Human Rights Commission, telling it that the rights of a huge mass of people were being violated. But even the NHRC did not respond. The governance and administration in UP will continue to be the worst in the country unless there is a political will to confront these problems and the aforementioned institutional mechanisms are put in place.

11 Governance of Uttar Pradesh

A Case Study For Effective Restructuring

Anand Sarup

Uttar Pradesh is at the threshold of a unique opportunity. After a very long time, a single party, the BSP, has come to power with an absolute majority and its leader, Chief Minister Mayawati, reigns supreme and unchallenged.

Any discussion regarding the problems of governance therefore, revolves around the fact that within the ambit of constitutional powers, Mayawati can do whatever she likes. Her limitations arise from her own priorities. Among these, the first is her ambition to assume power at the Centre and the second her commitment to reduce lawlessness. Finally, she has donned the mantle of inscrutability so as to be free from political inhibitions. Nobody really knows what she is truly committed to and this gives her the space to do what she wants and to choose the time for doing it.

Her ambition, motivated by a hard life, is to leave her imprint on the history of the state or perhaps, the nation. It appears that her political and bureaucratic advisors have developed the nimble foot of survival, capable of stepping off from anything which might arouse her ire. However powerful a crusader against casteism she may be, the lady is, after all, a product of that very same feudal casteist environment that still holds sway over middle India—UP, Bihar, Madhya Pradesh and Rajasthan.

There is a good possibility that she may one day play the prime ministerial role. If that be her ultimate objective, Mayawati first needs to get down to the business of stamping out the *ji-hazoori* variety of bad governance in the state for the uplift of its downtrodden masses, thus showing what she can do for the nation, should she become PM.

The question is whether she is interested in creating a democratic, inclusive, transparent and accountable system of governance in her state. That it can be done stands proven by UP's own very temporary achievement in the mid-70s, which will be discussed later in the chapter. This example shows that an open and transparent system, when it was introduced in planning, raised UP's growth rate to the top on the national list.

Unfortunately, the state government has a short institutional memory. One doesn't know whether Mayawati's attention has been drawn to the above facts, so as to let her try out some of the invaluable recipes. She is probably still unaware of them, as she continues harping on the unmanageable size of the state, demanding that the Centre speedily take steps for its trifurcation.

I am not willing to take a stand for or against the trifurcation demand, because such divisions does not necessarily lead to better governance. In fact, the opposite has been true in certain recent cases.

It is not clear as to whether her demand is politically motivated or she really thinks that UP is too big to be administered effectively. In any case, one can almost take it for granted that a decision either way will be based on political expediency.

Since the people are not yet in an agitation mode over the issue, there is enough time to reach a final decision after a detailed study of the pros and cons of trifurcation, such as the costs it would involve and the resulting benefits to the people in the three sub divisions, besides greater manageability in governance.

Both the state and the Centre needs to learn from the experience of the North-eastern states being cut up like a cake, as also of the creation of Uttarakhand, Jharkhand and Chhattisgarh in middle India. Nobody seems to have taken a hard look at—what the political, social and economic costs and benefits have been of these break ups. Actually, when you create a new political unit on the belief that it will lead to greater linguistic or ethnic coherence, you might end up creating more minorities within the new units and also reduce tolerance among the general populace for those who have now been made minorities. Look at what happened in Punjab to Hindus or is happening to the 'outsiders' in Maharashtra. Everybody expected the people of the hill areas to derive the maximum benefits from the creation of Uttarakhand but the people from the plains, viewed as outsiders earlier, have benefited more from the creation of this unit than the hill people. On the whole, bigger units with cultural compatibilities have greater capacity to absorb conflicts and contradictions.

It also needs to be recalled that Maharashtra, Andhra Pradesh, Rajasthan, Gujarat and even Karnataka have such irreconcilable disparities that their division would be far more justified than the division of UP. The whole idea of district planning got national currency because of the work started by Prof. Gadgil and people like Anna Sahib Sahasrabudhe in Vidharba region to counter the demand for subdivision of Maharashtra into five states. One recalls with pleasure the seminal work of Mr. D.G. Tungare for the development of a formula for distributing the state's divisible resources to the districts. Because of this and also because *Palak* ministers were appointed for each of the districts, Maharashtra remains undivided, not withstanding occasional bickerings.

In UP, we know that around 1975, something positive happened. Can we make it happen again? Here, it needs to be kept in mind that, by a Constitutional Amendment, Panchayati Raj institutions have now become key tiers in the scheme of national governance. If these units were provided with adequate funds and also invested with real power to take decisions, there would be no need to divide any state, because these units would be able to take care of the local priorities quite effectively.

To carry the argument foreward, it may be stated that division of a state is not the only way to improve performance. There is now as much scope for planning in specificity for a large state as there is for small states. Moreover, the proposal for division of UP has to be seen very carefully because, one of the downstream effects of this division would be interminable water rights disputes in an area which has a web of several rivers emanating from the same area, running through a vast land mass.

How Can a Planner Get to Work on Rational Planning for UP?

While the past Central and state governments have pursued total public sector or exclusively private investment, my government has decided to adopt a middle-path where we hope to attract private investment to improve the quality of our existing infrastructure. This, she assures would be done "without compromising with the interests of the existing employees and without surrendering the ownership of assets." These were the words of Mayawati at a press conference on 24 December 2007.

In the hands of a far seeing political advisor or an experienced planner, the above policy pronouncement would be quite adequate to initiate the formulation of policies which would go on to spell out the sectoral, spatial and temporal components of an integrated Plan for UP. This would necessarily evolve through point by point formulations based on the views, priorities and the specific goals articulated by the Chief Minster and her Cabinet.

Notwithstanding the expectation that there would be an unlimited inflow of public or private resources from outside, there is no getting away from the hard fact that a substantial proportion of resources will have to be raised, grimly and painstakingly, from the people of the state. At the same time, it has to be kept in mind that planning is not only about determining how and how much would be spent during a particular period but more importantly, it is about every *naya paisa* being well spent.

At this stage, one must take cognisance of the ORF Study Report prepared by Venkitesh Ramakrishnan, which states that:

> Over the entire period of the Five Year Plans the gap between national per capita income and that of the state has increased steadily. By 2001, per capita income in UP was 40% lower than the national average. Successive governments after independence have failed repeatedly to utilize state's considerable human and natural resources properly and efficiently. However, if the Fifth and Sixth Plans (1974-1985) were taken together UP's growth was around 9% per annum, which was significantly higher than that of the country as a whole (which stood at less than 6%). In the 1980s UP registered a growth rate in food grain production of 4.92%, which was much higher than the growth rate in the 70s. (37)

Just before the Sixth Plan was launched in 1977-78, UP's State Planning Institute, in a publication under the title *Planning for the Development of Uttar Pradesh*, in Chapter V, on "Reorienting the Planning Process", stated:

> The general feeling is that despite the tremendous expansion of economic or social infrastructure, the setting up basic industries with large capacities, extension of irrigation acilities and considerable increase in aggregates of agricultural production, the level and distribution of income has not registered a significant improvement. Obviously, to the extent this conclusion is valid, the situation call for serious introspection and the fashioning of appropriate investment policies, institutional mechanisms, administrative procedures, feedback arrangement and organisational changes required for mobilising public participation.

In the next Para 5.4., it added:

> In this context, it seems worthwhile recapitulating that for various reasons the actual rates of growth against stipulated projections have been consistently and considerably poor.

The relevant data is as follows:

Plan Period	*Targeted Growth Rate %*		*Actual Growth Rate %*	
	India	*UP*	*India*	*UP*
First Five Year Plan			3.8	1.9
Second Five Year Plan			3.2	1.8
Third Five Year Plan	Over 5		3.2	1.8
Three Annual Plans	5.5	5.6	3.5	2.6
Fifth Five Year Plan (First two years 1974-1976)	....	.....	3.4	5.5

The sole objective of how, during the first two years of the Fifth Plan, UP managed to register a higher growth rate than the nation's average is to point out that there is nothing inherently wrong with Uttar Pradesh. In spite of its internal disparities and a feudal culture, it did demonstrate over a four-year period that Uttar Pradesh is governable and its economic development too can be accelerated.

Reorienting Up's Planning Process of Planning and Development

With the Eleventh Five Year Plan taking shape under a new political order, it is necessary to determine whether some steps can be taken to recreate the environment for accelerated development which gave unusually good results between 1974 and 1976. In the late 1960s the planning process was reoriented largely on the recommendations of the then Deputy Chairman of the Planning Commission, Prof. D.R.Gadgil on the preconditions and the processes of development. One of his basic beliefs was that, in planning, everything is related to everything else in a space-time-function continuum. This makes the planning process too complicated to be undertaken only in abstract terms, mainly by manipulating financial forces. The neat equations on paper fail to work when put in to practice—that is, when one tries to figure out its impact in various areas and sectors, in a multilevel context.

He laid great store by the processes of multilevel consultation, insisting that, to be really useful, consultation and reflection should be in a transparent environment, without a disorienting sense of hierarchy or the existence of any kind of apprehensions in the minds of participants. These negative elements, he felt, invariably curtail freedom of thought and expression. During the short period in which he served as the Deputy Chairman of the Planning Commission, he made a signal contribution by:

(a) Ending the hegemony of the Central Ministries in the matter of planning by doing away with their long catalogues of schematic patterns of loan-grant components;

(b) Releasing the creativity of states by formulating an objective and aggregative formula for the distribution Central assistance (now called the Gadgil Formula) allowing states, for the first time, to draw their due share of the assistance even when they refused to submit their plans to the Planning Commission; and

(c) Disciplining the Central Ministries by putting limits on the huge diversions of disposable funds from the assistance pool into centrally

> sponsored schemes, thus encouraging the concerned ministries to tempt rather than convince the states to do exactly what they would have done if they were spending their own money, in pursuance of a particular Plan objective. He realised that anyone can make mistakes and admitted that, in the Mid-term Appraisal of the Fourth Five Year Plan itself, the formula for distribution of Central assistance that he himself had crafted had fallen short of the norms of equity.

One must put an end to this panegyric about what lessons his life and work holds for the planners by reminding his successors that, like Socrates, he preferred a cup of hemlock and got sacked unceremoniously, rather than bow to policies he perceived as arbitrary, elitist or out of sync with the approaches he had evolved with the advice of the National Development Council.

One of the outcomes of Prof. Gadgil's advocacy for a new paradigm for state planning was an emphasis on capacity building by the state governments for undertaking state and district planning. In due course, schemes were drawn up assuring liberal grants to state governments for recruiting and training statisticians, economists, project planners, evaluators, etc. Predictably, this dispensation helped Uttar Pradesh create a planning organisation, commensurate with its size and the complexity of its problems.

Some of the institutions created with the resources for strengthening the planning machinery were: the State Planning Commission, an Economic Advisory Committee and a Public Investment Board, under the auspices of a well staffed State Planning Institute. As a corollary to the recognition that reviews of plan implementation was as important as finding extra resources for the plans, a decision was taken to set up an all powerful Cabinet Sub-Committee for Monitoring Plan Implementation.

Very few people are aware of the conspiratorial manner in which the first moves were made for the wholesale restructuring of UP's planning process. Those were the days of emergency and everything suggested by or on behalf of the then PM was taken as law by all Chief Ministers, including Narayan Dutt Tewari. One of the principal conspirators for the establishment of an independent, transparent and highly accomplished planning system in UP was none other than Mr. P.N. Haksar, then Deputy Chairman of the National Planning Commission. Because of his excellent equation with Mr. P.N. Haksar, the then planning secretary was able to convince him that UP was not making the progress it could, because of the feudal culture, in which nobody spoke up for fear of displeasing his or her political or bureaucratic masters.

This dialogue resulted in Mr. P.N. Haksar and the planning secretary drawing up a broad plan and a conspiratorial stratagem for putting pressure on UP's Chief Minister for restructuring the process as well as the organisation for planning. The process of the stratagem is shown in the arrowed boxes below:

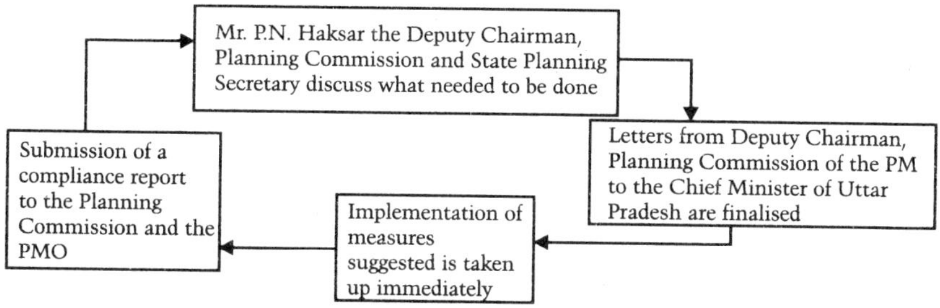

As soon as the process of restructuring of the planning process got under way, it became apparent that nothing would be gained unless something drastic was done to save the planning process from the sycophants and bureaucrats who did not understand the first principles of free discussion.

That is why an Economic Advisory Committee was set up, with a composition that convinced everybody that its members would express themselves freely, without bothering about their perception of what the Chief Ministers and others in power wanted to hear. Looking back, one wonders how the Chief Minister and his Cabinet colleagues agreed to appoint people, mostly outsiders, as reputed for their formidable academic prowess as for their articulate independence. One recalls with pleasure how Raja Chelliah, Suresh Tendulkar, Y.K. Alag, A.M. Khusro, G.S. Bhalla and several others agreed to join the Advisory Committee and participated in evolving polices. They chaired committees that reviewed programmes and projects and gave status reports to the Cabinet Sub-Committee for Monitoring Plan Implementation.

One of the reasons for creating the sub-committee was the realisation that there was no point going to great lengths to secure more resources for the state plans unless it was also ensured that all the key projects and programmes would be completed quickly enough to yield substantial benefits within the shortest possible time.

Accordingly, a list of key projects and programmes was drawn up and every three months, the Planning Department presented a report to the sub-committee on the time overruns and also worked out the costs of delays in terms of postponement of returns, etc. The sub-committee did take immediate decisions to seek clarifications and also, where necessary, passed immediate orders to remove the snags. This led to the formulation of reports on 'Cost of Delays in Decision Making' which made at least two Chief Ministers ask, whenever the occasion arose, as to what would be the cost of their postponing a particular decision. Another outcome was the monitoring of the budget percentage spent during the four quarters of the financial year, resulting in documentation of the waste and financial irregularities. This sometimes ended in the reduction or enhancement of outlays for some projects after the first six months of the year.

The cumulative results of these measures, as noted earlier, was that UP raced ahead of the national average in annual income growth. It is obvious that regular reviews of the cost of time overruns in the completion of projects and programmes brought about a general consciousness of how even a short delay can be far more expensive than the appointment of some extra personnel. It also resulted in more specific detailing of the plans for the inflow of various inputs and the likely outflow of various benefits, while drawing up project and plans before putting these up for the approved of the State's Public Investment Board.

There were other benefits besides the direct gains from the plan reorientation. The interactions among independent and articulate academicians of national stature infused, many of the UP bureaucrats with a new sense of self-confidence and also an independent viewpoint on the process of development. The academicians, on their part, became much more aware of the internal and external compulsions under which UP had to labour for growth.

Eventually, the State Planning Institute produced a small but telling booklet for the 33rd meeting of the National Development Council. Its bar diagrams showed at a glance how the flows of Central government to UP had been much lower than those to the developed states. This presentation persuaded the Prime Minister to review the Gadgil Formula and later to adopt its modified version, incorporating the element of Income Adjusted Total Population. This resulted in the considerable increase of plan resources for UP, Bihar and some other backward states.

Where Do We Go from Here?

To decide upon how one would go about the business of gingering up the processes of planning and development in UP, one would have to review what was done to reorient these processes when the Sixth Five Year Plan was on the anvil. Besides Narayan Dutt Tewari, there were other people on the scene, including Mr. Tribuwan Prasad, a most supportive Finance Secretary, Mr. D.P. Octania, Director of Economics and Statistics, Dr. B.C. Das, the veteran evaluator, Satya Prakash, with his invaluable forthright advice and IAS officers like A.K. Dar, J.L. Bajaj, Prabhu Ghate, etc., who were willing to work till the wee hours of the morning, for an idea and a strategy they hoped would deliver the goods for UP.

At a later stage, people like Madhukar Dighe and Ram Naresh Yadav, the Chief Minster and the Finance Minister appeared on the scene. Their integrity far outweighed their sense of self importance and commitment to UP's development. In spite of the fact that Narayan Dutt Tewari, Madhukar Dighe and Ram Naresh Yadav were intensely political persons, they were willing to leave the business of planning and the monitoring of plan implementation to people who were indisputably without any political or bureaucratic ambitions. They were able to do what needed to be done because they were not looking for a quick promotion. One of their strengths flowed from their willingness to quit any position when they realised that they had reached the end of the road.

Even now, if one has to come up with a viable plan of action for resuscitation of the processes of planning and development, one would have to search hard for personages of such calibre and integrity—people who have the humility to admit that it is practically impossible to know, at the starting point, all that needs to be done for evolving a new strategy but are prepared to learn on way, exploring facts as well as the scope for improvement.

It is essential to restrain oneself from the old man's folly of waffling about generalities and instead stick to speaking in terms of one, two, three of what, where and how one might start work. But faced with this challenge, one would do well to start with figuring out why UP is not progressing as fast and as purposefully as it must. This is one subject on which many people have made their surmises. It would be necessary to get all such people, from all walks of life, involved in colloquia to establish some sort of a broad consensus on the reasons for UP's backwardness, not only in broad socio-economic terms but also in sector-specific terms, paying due attention to important social, technological and organisational indicators.

The biggest problem, it appears, would be in finding people who would speak out the truth without fear of reprisals. But if some of the discussions are held, initially in non-political forums outside Uttar Pradesh, some knowledgeable persons might come out with their candid views and in the process we may discover what ails the state and then come up with some remedial ideas.

In this context, we need to note that India has changed radically between 1970 and 2008. The situations are as different as chalk and cheese, in terms of global dynamics, technological potentials and education.

It should be obvious from this fact that any plan of action for UP's development must take a dynamic rather than a static view of today's processes of development. For this again, we will have to get the help from experts from outside, who do not depend for their survival on UP's politicians and bureaucrats. For this, we will have to pay recognition or consultancy fees—whatever they want, following Peter Ducker's view that an ounce of reflection is more valuable than a tonne of blind and unreflecting experience.

Quite possibly, some bankers, entrepreneurs, NGOs, academics, intrepid civil servants or UP's own development planners would come forward to help. One needs to talk to such people because they are the ones who know what at this point of time can wake up the state with the kiss of life to revitalise the state's financial, technological and managerial system out of its cosy state of self-satisfaction. Once UP wakes, it will be able to dictate its own terms and in the process, assume a position of leadership in the country.

It is difficult to imagine UP's official organs taking charge at this political juncture, coming to grips with the processes of plan reorientation.To initiate this process, perhaps an ad hoc mechanism without a political label would have to be set up with the backing of a well funded virtual organisation for 'Exploring for UP's Accelerated Socio-Economic Development'. Considering the circumstances, it is essential that the proposed mechanism should start with an agenda to which no one can reasonably object and which cannot be misinterpreted as a veiled move to play politics. It is also essential to find resources for the proposed mechanism from an organisation which does not have a questionable reputation. How these things have to be managed can be learned from the mid-1970s story of how people just ignored outdated notions about paying people to come to UP and contribute their time and wisdom to speed up its development.

At the initial stage, it was presumed that the Finance Department would not agree to the expense involved in inviting outside consultants or members of the Economic Advisory Committee. The guests would travel by air, get a daily allowance of Rs. 2000 per month, have a taxi at their beck and call all through their stay at the newly set up 'Clark's Avadh' Hotel in Lucknow. However, Dr. Kamla Chowdhry, who was then working with the Ford Foundation, found an ingenious solution. She got a commitment from the Foundation that if the claim of a person's travel, board, lodging and other costs were endorsed even verbally by an informally designated officer of UP government, the Ford Foundation would make direct reimbursements of whatever they were entitled to the claimant. When this arrangement was being discussed, it was assumed that once the scheme got going, it would be possible to get the state government to accept that the experts being appointed to the Economic Advisory Committee be paid at the rates agreed to by the Ford Foundation. And very soon this came true.

This point is being made here to underline that, over the years, people with ideas and expertise have become conscious of the value of their time. Some of them may ask to be paid five, ten or even fifteen thousand rupees per day for their time of stay in UP. After all, the World Bank's personnel and the Directors on the Boards of private firms and also some public enterprises are being paid a lot in the form of DA and other perks.

The following is a conceptual framework of a Centre which might be set up, initially outside the purview of the UP government, to explore and develop scenarios for the accelerated development of UP. It is firmly believed that in about a year, this framework would get adopted by the UP government.

Conceptual Framework for a Virtual Centre or Accelerated Development of Uttar Pradesh

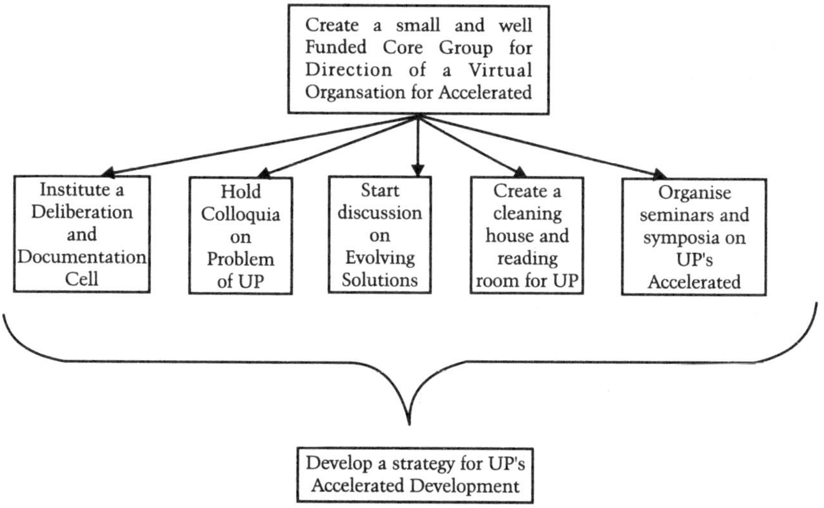

A virtual organisation has many advantages over a normal bureaucratic organisation. It comes into being as a task force and disappears when the task is done. It does not create permanent liabilities or commitments *vis-a-vis* the staff and does not lead, in the long run, to management being asked to create avenues of promotion for people, irrespective of their contribution, on the specious plea that they had put in so many years with the organisation.

Even in the 70s, when the 'dream job' notions about the IAS had not yet fully disappeared, the government of Uttar Pradesh agreed to make tenure appointment for: Advisor, Economic Planning; Specialist, Technical appraisal; Specialist, Project Formulation and Appraisal; and Specialist, Financial Appraisal with emoluments in excess of the package received by the Chief Secretary of Uttar Pradesh.

It was in pursuance of this new approach, that the Planning Department also floated a Planning and Management Consultancy and Data Systems Corporation, which was later rechristened as UP Development Systems Corporation, chiefly because, unlike Maharashtra, Gujarat, West Bengal, Tamil Nadu and Karnataka, at that time UP did not have any consultancy organisations or academic institutions on the pattern of Tata Consultancy Services or the Administrative Staff College and the institutes of management.

While proposing the setting up of a 'virtual organisation' for initiating the study of UP's problems and developing data based view points about how to lift the state out of the morass of backwardness, one might, like Alice in Wonderland, begin from the beginning and carry on to the end. For a start, one might list the objectives which would have to be given the highest priority, recognising that at this stage, it is best to be flexible about allowing new items to be included as and when necessary. Some of the things which come straight to mind are:

(a) The primacy of establishing the rule of law which would not discriminate between people on the basis of caste, creed, economic status, political affiliations, etc., and in the process, create an environment of security and freedom from fear;

(b) Taking steps to enforce effective and expeditious relief under the Right to Information Act;

(c) Giving due priority to providing qualitatively comparable education in all kinds of public and private schools;

(d) Eliminating corruption caused by avoidable delays in the conduct of public and private business; and

(e) Evaluating systems put in place in 1975-76 under auspices of the state's Planning and Development Systems to discover how these are performing and also what these can contribute through some managerial resuscitation.

Besides looking for ways to deal with the above issues, work will have to be taken up to discover, for the state as a whole and also in disaggregated terms, the present status of the state in matter of economic, social, cultural and administrative development. Besides this, opinion surveys will have to be conducted to discover what image Uttar Pradesh has in the eyes of overseas investment agencies, dynamic banking institutions and also among young graduates from IITs and IIMs (as an employment destination). It would be pointless to prepare an inventory of questions for study all by oneself. The initial agenda has to be very flexible and open ended for additions when necessary. The road ahead for UP is clear. Get on with the task systematically, starting from any point in the long and undistinguished history of UP's plodding on the path of socio-economic development. For surely, it is better to light a candle than curse the darkness.

12 Using Technology to Improve Governance

R.R. Shah

Any analysis of the governance in Uttar Pradesh must take into consideration the fact that the State's performance in financial resource mobilisation was generally good in the financial years from 2006 to 2008. In 2007-08, instead of an overdraft, they had a positive balance of about Rs. 5000 crore. The positive result was seen in plan funding, which improved enormously. The area that needs to be criticised is finance management, as it carried forward the positive balances without expending them on the allocated projects. In my four year tenure in the Planning Commission, I have witnessed the plan funds increase from around Rs. 7000-8000 crore half a decade ago to Rs. 25000 crore in 2007-2008.

This happened because resources were available—it was more fortuitous than deliberate. The Centre's resources from tax collection had shown a buoyant rise of over 15 per cent nationwide and in the disbursement of that sum to the states, UP received the largest amount. It was the largest recipient of the 12th Finance Commission award. The state's own sales tax revenues have been very buoyant and Noida, being a part of the National Capital Region (NCR), registered a very high rate of stamp duty. The general trend has been that, even though the stamp duty rates have gone down, its income as well as that of excise duty have gone up. Sales tax has been showing a buoyancy of over 20 per cent. In a nutshell, UP has the resources to do what needs to be done and there is a qualitative difference in the scenario as compared to what it was four years back.

The pity is that the actual physical delivery does not keep pace with the progress on the financial front. Going by social indicators, such as health or education or core sectors like agriculture, the state's performance is appalling. Put simply, the increases in revenue are not reflected on the actual growth figures, which is still under 5-6 per cent. One can, at present, only hope that the state will start coming up to the national level. But it must also be noted that there was a time when UP was averaging only around 4 per cent growth. There has been hardly any investment in agriculture and irrigation during the last 10 years or so. Industry is also not developing and the investment climate, as is well known, is not very conducive. Probably, all that UP is thriving upon is the fact that it is a trading junction for goods being sent from Delhi to Bihar and Madhya Pradesh, etc. Probably this commercial exchange is bringing some prosperity. The other aspect is the burgeoning of public spending, best illustrated in Lucknow, where more beautiful buildings are coming up than in any other state capital. But there is credibility to the common belief that most of the real estate fund is slush money. It is parallel economy at its best.

After setting out this broad background, this chapter seeks to highlight how governance can be streamlined, especially by the use of technology. The focus of this chapter relates to the government's interface with citizens, as also with the business world. If we can take care of these two aspects, i.e., G2C and G2B domains, then we will have done a signal service to the state. The first step in this direction would be to improve the services and programme deliveries of the government through the instruments of information technology (IT), as far as possible avoiding the time consuming conventional methods. A fine example would be the IT-based e-Seva, where the service station is manned by a private provider and not a government person. In his interface with the people, he has no control over the records on the basis of which he is delivering these services, so he cannot 'doctor' the data. Since those with the power to alter records do not have a face to face contact with the public, a very welcome cut is made in the circuit of corruption. Before the days of the IT revolution and the more recent Right to Information Act, the bureaucrat who controlled the records also dealt directly with the information seeking public. He, therefore, had the discretion to play with the records and thus extort money from the hapless information seeker. e-Seva, therefore, can be considered a technological pioneer in the task of curing UP governance of its worst ailment—corruption. Law and order is another area where IT can help enormously. During my tenure as the Principal Home Secretary, this was the area I was working on and I was able to create a Special Task Force (STF). The STF was based on superior fire-power, superior mobility, superior communication ability and power to intercept. The STF has recorded some astounding successes in those days. It still is considered to be one of the more effective anti-mafia forces. If we look at the law and order situation in its totality, one can see that aspects such as perpetration of crime, registration, investigation, prosecution, adjudication and incarceration is a continuum. Now, IT can be used to keep track of a crime from the time it is committed by giving it a particular ID number and follow it right up to the adjudication and incarceration stage. IT would help you know exactly what is being done about the crime that has been committed, whether the perpetrators have been punished. This kind of start-to-finish knowledge is just not possible through the old pen and paper record-keeping ways of the police. Technology enables you to create an integrated information database, which allows you a total view.

Let us go a step further. The same database can produce information on criminal history sheets, which can then be fortified by using finger print lifting equipment at all police stations, as is being done in advanced countries. There, the police precincts lift the fingerprint using the equipment and it goes straight into the central database, from where you can instantly call up the history sheet on to the computer screen by just pressing a few keys. There are, of course further biometric refinements, such as the DNA printing and retinal recognition, besides whatever surprise technology has in store for us.

IT offers very easy solutions, through Radio Frequency Identification (RFID), to problems like absenteeism by school teachers or congestion at the toll barriers. An RFID on the windscreen of your car means that your number is instantly recognised and recorded and if you have the easy pass, you simply have to just sign and pass through. This would reduce the long queues at the toll barriers. The technique is as simple for schools. The teacher is given the RFID. The transmitting and the recording stations are both at the school. You will know precisely how long the teacher was in school and the duration should be made the basis of his salary. No system is perfect, but this would at least ensure that the teacher does not get free bees even when he was not physically present in school. Both the awareness and use of these and other technologies should be encouraged in governance as it would help bring growth into the fast forward mode. There is a whole chapter on e-Governance in the 11th Five Year Plan paper.

When you refer to G2C and G2B—that is government's interface with citizen's businesses—you are actually talking about two kinds of unique identifiers. The first is a magnetic medium identifier in the G2C domain called Unique ID, projected for every citizen or resident of India. This is a project which is already being implemented and acquiring some shape. As many as 67 crore residents of India have been given these IDs. Its remarkable benefit is that all the development plans, including anti-poverty programmes, can be delivered at the individual level, addressing the ID recipients concerns at a more personalised and more efficient level. Most of these programmes are currently being delivered village-wise, sprinkling funds on a 'spray and pray' basis. The rather quaint modus operandi was to throw away the funds at the village and hope for the best. With the IT method, you can create conduits that would lead to each individual beneficiary. A common unique identity can eventually be turned into a smartcard. That common unique ID could be used for health programmes, National Rural Health Mission (NRHM) programmes, education, agriculture subsidies, fertiliser subsidies and whatever other areas that may be identified. A unique ID would let you know the exact quantum of assistance that is actually being delivered to the target beneficiary, thus substantially reducing the chances of it getting misdirected. This is the advantage of a unique identifier on the citizen's domain.

Let us look at the unique identifier for the businesses. The Company Law Department already has implemented a project called MCA21 with great success. It was given in the form of company identification numbers (CIN) to 700,000 industrial establishments in the country in the corporate sector. It has enabled the corporate units to e-file their returns either to the Company Law Department or to the SEBI. All corporate returns can be e-filed now. So, you have provided the businesses with an automatic interface on an anytime anywhere basis, doing away with the bother of going to government offices. For those small businesses that cannot write out their own returns, there are interface centres where they are provided assistance of chartered accountants and legal experts to enable them to file their returns. This will bring about a major difference on the businesses-government interface. There is a National e-Governance Programme, which has 21 mission mode projects in the ambit of the 11th Plan. These projects relate to income tax, excise, customs, insurance, banking, pensions and passports. About 10 of them come under the Central government, 7 or 8 under the state governments and 5 to 6 programmes such as e-Commerce and e-Biz, are integrated programmes involving both the Central and the state governments.

As is evident, technology enables the government to come up with a system which is integrated. The citizens' interface with the government can be on a citizen's portal and with the businesses an e-Biz portal. This is conceptually possible. The UP Government needs to be sensitised to these possibilities contained in the 11th Plan document. That could help it to overcome some of the problems which have confounded its machinery all these years. Of course, e-Governance is not a panacea for all ills and certainly a lot more will be required to take care of the behavioural and moral aspects, but at least efficiency-related aspects can be taken care of through e-Governance.

IV

Regionalism in Uttar Pradesh: A Case for Reorganisation of State

13 Regional Disparities in UP and the Case for Reorganisation

Gyanesh Kudaisya

This chapter takes a historical approach to Uttar Pradesh and not a geopolitical point of view or a regional development and planning perspective. It looks at the state in terms of its prominence as a region, in terms of its identity as a 'political heartland' of the country. The effort is to historically situate the region that is called Uttar Pradesh today. Secondly, the chapter seeks to question its identity as the 'heartland'. It would also seek to revisit the issue of reorganisation because it has a history going back to the early 1950s. It will touch upon all the debates and arguments that have been made for and against dividing Uttar Pradesh. There is also the need to broaden this discussion to pan-Indian dimentions, so as to examine how the state's reorganisations have taken place in their four phases or the four key episodes.

Uttar Pradesh as a political entity goes back to the British period. The British conquest of Northern India was a gradual process. The process began with the eastern most districts of Mirzapur, Jaunpur in the late 18th century and continued steadily up to the revolt of 1857, when the last part of the region, the kingdom of Awadh was annexed. This political entity, which was created through a process of colonial conquest, was a constructed entity. The region was conquered or annexed and bundled into one unit for administrative convenience. The entity, therefore, comprises very disparate areas spread over this vast land mass, starting from Gorakhpur-Banaras in the east and through Bundelkhand to the Awadh area in the west, all put together by the Raj, to be first named the 'North Western Province' and later the 'United Provinces of Agra and Awadh'. The renaming itself suggests that there was, at least, the notion that the vast region was actually two provinces, with Agra and Awadh being the western wing. Even the British could not be blind to the huge difference between the permanently settled eastern most *zamindari* districts and those in the western end of the larger construct they had created. The first assumption we therefore, come to is that what came into being and exists to date is a constructed identity as a region.

If we examine the regional differentiations, not only in UP but in the rest of the nation and study the literature that has evolved over the notion of regions—both in a general theoretical sense and in relation to India—they seem to suggest that the regions, as they have come to exist today are not their real identities. These are entities constructed within the geopolitical parameters of the time. There is convincing literature which suggests that the regions' primordial and existential continuum have been broken and that they have not been formed by natural environment. Regions are social constructs; regions are constructed in space and time. These constructions give particular meanings, particular place identities and particular social identities to regions and this happens through a geo-historical process. So regions have been constructed through a process of history, evolving over time into nation states. Not fixed in time, they are subject to change and their identity undergoes mutations and revisions.

In the study of regional differentiation, one must factor in its natural resources, languages or dialects and the dominant elites, some of which have been formed by them. Bundela Rajputs have played a powerful role in shaping Bundelkhand's history and shaping its identity. Also to be considered are the social (caste) structure, the land and revenue systems, and the cultural practices. Socialist leader Ram Manohar Lohia had pointed out that while Hindus in UP's east are *Rambhakts* those in the west are devotees of Krishna. Anthropologist Bernard Cohen has listed 18 different attributes that contribute to the making of a region. These include a whole range of factors. For example, marriage networks and a whole range of related factors could be brought in to play.

Uttar Pradesh has been seen as a political heartland, which has had a key role in shaping the history of the 20th century India. But this is a multiple, overlapping identity about which we can formulate six types of constructions. Perhaps the first could be to consider it as a Hindu heartland. The region has the two sacred rivers Yamuna and Ganga, the main pilgrim centres of Badrinath, Kedarnath, Haridwar, Mathura, Varanasi. This has led the mass psyche to look upon the region as the *Aryavrat*, the core or the soul of Hinduism.

But at the same time, there is also its construct as a "Muslim Heartland". It has the great centres of Indo-Islamic urban life, such as Lucknow, kingdom of Awadh, the Muslim kingdom of Jaunpur and of course, the Babri Masjid. Right from the east to west of the state, there is a plethora of Muslim place names. This region has had a strong Indo-Islamic associations even before the the Mughal reign. The heyday of that culture was in the declining years of the Mughal empire, with the emergence of Awadh as an important regional kingdom as well as the princely state of Rampur. There are also the well established Muslim seminaries of Deoband, Firangi Mahal and Nadhwa. Then there is the important role the Muslim elite played in the burgeoning of India's Islamic culture, such as the launching of the Aligarh movement, creating and refining the Urdu language and, indeed in giving an impetus to the campaign for the Pakistan movement. These are all vital elements in the creation of the state's identity.

Then, to examine the 20th century constructions we need to begin with the colonial construction of the state in the late 19th century. After the conquest of Awadh, following the 1857 revolt, the British consolidated their rule in North West Province and created basic institutions through the land revenue system, urban system and policing—extending the criminal justice system to the countryside by developing close relationships with landlords. They basically created what they called a model province. There were two model provinces in the British times—Punjab and United Provinces—and the colonial rulers believed the latter to be one of the best directly ruled provinces of British India and thereby grew the notion that it was the heartland of their reign. In their decision in 1911 to relocate the Capital of India from Calcutta to New Delhi, one can see that an important factor was its the proximity of UP, the 'heartland'.

Then, you have the pioneers of the freedom struggle, the nationalists' takeover of this heartland. It began in the 1920s and continued to the 1940s, as it became the central arena of the freedom struggle. It was spearheaded by the Congress Party, the most powerful organisation that launched the great campaigns for peasant mobilisation. It is not a coincidence that the headquarters of the Indian National Congress was located at Allahabad rather than in Delhi. The Congress had succeeded in virtually taking over this heartland through its mobilisation and the province contributed the largest number of political prisoners in all the campaigns from 1920 till 1947.

Then came the post-colonial construction of UP and the different building blocks of that identity. In the most recent times, the state has been politically reconstructed as a Dalit heartland. In the ongoing process, the present belongs to Mayawati—with her contribution not just to history but to geography. One obvious proof of Dalit dominance are the names with strong Buddhist associations given to some new and old districts, such as Shravasti, Kapilvastu, Gautam Budh Nagar, to name just three of several others.

In the late 40s and early 50s, the post-colonial leaders debated about three very basic issues concerning the new construction of UP's identity. The first was the name 'United Provinces' itself: what would be the appropriate name for the state? The second was about what its official language should be and the third dealt with its territorial boundaries. So, the first issue was of renaming of Uttar Pradesh. There were as many as 20 suggestions. Some said the old name, the United Provinces could be retained but it was rejected out of hand. Some offered a kind of translated name, such as 'Samyukt Prant' in Hindi or 'Muttahada' in Urdu, but they were found not really acceptable. The favourite name was 'Aryavrat'.

In 1947, the issue was debated in the UP Legislative Council and in the UP Cabinet. In 1948, about 96 members of the UPCC met and unanimously chose the name 'Aryavrat'. This included people like Govind Ballabh Pant himself. The proposal was sent to the Constituent Assembly in Delhi which was then finalising the names of the new provinces. Even though the UP leadership was unanimous on this name, the Central leadership—with Nehru playing the key role—at the last minute managed to stop it from being renamed as 'Aryavrat'.

Then the question of language. UP had a major role to play in making Hindi the national language. It is through UP that Hindi came to be associated, if not identified, with the freedom struggle. Premchand and many other great writers and poets came from UP and the literary centres of the language were in Benares and Allahabad. But the issue was not just about Hindi. There was a strong demand that Urdu be made the second language in UP, to which there was an equally strong opposition. Unfortunately, the entire spectrum of UP leadership was completely sold on not just Hindi but on an exclusive, purist version of the language. The southern states put up a strong resistance to this sanskriticised and brahminical style of language. It was also an element that added to the feeling of alienation among the Muslims. In many ways, the UP leadership played a leading role in installing Hindi as a national language. It led the Nagri campaign of the 40s and the 50s. At the central level, it played a key role in reforming the script and creating the earliest lexicons of official words, among other things—thereby enthroning of Hindi as a national language.

The third issue, that is fixing UP's territorial boundaries, has to be considered in the context of post-Independence reorganisation of the states. There are four episodes which are involved in this. The first is the 1954-1956 period during which the States Reorganisation Commission worked. The second is the 1966 Haryana-Punjab bifurcation. The third is the north-eastern states which were created in 1972 and most recently, the 2000 creation of three new states.

Let us begin with the States Reorganisation Commission. Reorganisation of states was then a highly emotive issue, particularly in southern India where the old Madras state which consisted of Malayali, Tamil, Kannada, Telugu speakers, were all lumped together within one administrative unit. The demand for the creation of four southern states was voiced right after Independence and to this was added the Gujarati and Marathi agitations. These were highly emotive campaigns. Though the Congress had committed itself to the linguistic principle in 1920 itself, it balked at the idea of any changes just after the horror of the Partition blood bath. The Central leadership was totally focused on the single aim of keeping the nation intact after half of Bengal and Punjab had been sliced off to create East and West Pakistan. New Delhi firmly decided to go slow with the reorganisation process so as not to allow linguistic sentiments to arouse divisive passions and intentions. But such passions were indeed, aroused when Andhra activist Potti Sriramulu died 56 days after he went on an indefinite fast. Three days of rioting erupted in that part of Madras state which is today Andhra Pradesh and massive campaigns were launched in Madras, Bombay and Gujarat. Nehru had to bow to such strong grass roots demand. Andhra Pradesh came into being in 1953 and the States Reorganisation Commission was appointed. It is in the context of this time of turmoil, partition fallouts and high passions that the UP boundaries issue has to be studied. In 1953, the Delhi State Assembly passed a resolution for taking the Rohilkhand, Agra and Meerut divisions out of UP and incorporating it with Delhi, thereby creating a new Delhi state. Western UP MLAs numbering 112 supported the move with great enthusiasm and 96 of them signed a memorandum which was presented before the SRC without even Chief Minister G.B. Pant knowing anything about it. When apprised of what had transpired, Pant came down heavily on the MLAs, saying the action was tantamount to sedition on the part of the Congress legislators. A meeting was called in Lucknow at which Pant made his famous speech to the effect that no power on earth could "divide this land of Ram and Krishna", this "heartland". New Delhi supported his argument because it looked upon UP as a counter weight to the linguistic pressures it was under. So, while the south got its four states, UP was told it could exist with its size and diversity as one unit and it would be a counter weight to an overemphasis on linguistic principles. They were, after all, not absolute principles.

Keeping its territories intact, the UP leadership basically consolidated its position as a political heartland. All in all, some can argue that UP is the bastion of the national language—'Hindi of Hindustan'—and the 'political heartland' of the nation in the sense that it has the largest number of parliamentarians, as also a high percentage of political leaders with national status.

What the states' reorganisation basically did was to give India six new states—four in the south and two in the west—after a lot of opposition and experiencing a deep sense of uncertainty both at the Central and the provincial level. There were very powerful movements and there were intensely contested issues that had to be dealt with. For example, between 1955 and 1960, there was the nagging question as to who should get Bombay. Finding no answers, they first made it into a bilingual state in 1956, but finding this untenable, they apportioned the state between Maharashtra and Gujarat and the city of Bombay was handed over to Maharashtra. It can be seen that, from 1920 to 1960, it was linguistic sentiments that activated the Indians. Things have moved on since then.

Sikh aspirations for a state of their own had a lot to do with the bifurcation of Punjab to create Haryana in 1996. Actually the aim was to accommodate the Sikhs who fundamentally wanted a state based on their religion. But to avoid any communalistic overtones, the bifurcation was carried out in the garb of linguistic principles. Then came the the creation of states on the basis of ethnicity in the north-east. But this is a different story altogether. The need arose not because of any grassroots movements but because of a revolutionary change in New Delhi's thinking after the trauma of the Chinese invasion in 1963. Nagaland was created right after the war in 1963 to prevent secessionism from getting out of control. Within a decade full statehood was given to Meghalaya, Manipur and Tripura, while Mizoram and Arunachal Pradesh were recognised as union territories in 1973. This is really the larger state responding to the imperatives of security to create new states on ethnic considerations, as today's map of the North-east clearly illustrates.

At the turn of the century came the formation of three new states—Chhattisgarh, Uttaranchal and Jharkhand—with the latter two's demands going back to the 40s. These were really marginalised and neglected regions. Chhattisgarh did not even have a very strong movement for statehood but it benefited from the electoral games certain parties played. In all this, we see the coming to the fore of federalism. First, there were the language considerations in the south and the west, overtones of religion in the north, then the ethnic divide in the north-east and finally the marginalised and neglected regions in middle India.

This chapter has attempted to give a historical background and appreciation of the demands for the creation of Harit Pradesh, Bundelkhand and Poorvanchal. Those making these demands today will have to think about how to build a regional identity and agenda. The UP leadership has not done this. In the 60 years since Independence, it has neither evolved a regional identity nor agenda. None of its great leaders have truly been regional leaders, even though they were national leaders. As soon as they come to the forefront they begin to look at the Centre. Whether he be Pandit Gobind Ballabh Pant or Lal Bahadur Shastri, or any one else. Compare that to the leaders from Gujarat or Tamil Nadu who, when they joined the Central government, make it apoint to speak for their states for they essentially represent states that have a very cohesive regional identity and regional agenda. This is completely missing if you look at UP's political history.

In the present situation there are certain positives that needs to be highlighted. For one thing, there is none of the emotive indulgence in any of the three new demands. There is no single protagonist, no single champion—no Potti Sriramulu willing to fast to death for the creation of any of these states. This is indeed a great advantage. It is possible to approach this question rationally so as to deal the region's backwardness through good planning. Then there is an absence of intra-regional conflict. You don't have the Cauvery-Tamil Nadu kind of conflict. These demands, therefore, can be approached by first giving primacy to developmental considerations. What we really need are not new states, but new types of states. If these states come into being they must move away from the heartland's administrative and ideological legacies. They must be representative, decentralised and inclusive. Their primary task has to be to inculcate regional loyalty and formulate a regional agenda. This cannot simply happen by breaking up states. The state structures have to re-scale themselves and this is a very important part. In the last 20 years the discourse on decentralisation has gone further. The effort should be to build those decentralised initiatives that have been attempted but not concretised on the ground. In the final analysis, it is not new states but new types, or rather new quality of states that need to be considered.

14 Politics of Harit Pradesh

The Case of Western UP as a Separate State

Jagpal Singh

The elite in a democratic polity manipulate both extant as well as constructed issues and symbols for mobilising support. The demand for a separate or an autonomous state is an example of such attempts. Creation of three new states, i.e., Jharkhand, Uttaranchal and Chhattisgarh in November 2000 has given boost to such demands in other parts of the country. The demand for the separation of western UP to create 'Harit Pradesh' is one of the latest cases. Such demands are usually made for the relatively backward areas. Western UP's politicians are touting their region's prosperity as the reason for their demand. The prosperity aspect may have parallels with Punjab but the dissimilarities between the two are more glaring than the commonalities.

This chapter attempts to analyse certain issues relating to the demand for a Harit Pradesh, comprising certain western districts of UP. It argues that the demand is intertwined in the caste dominated politics of the region. It is spearheaded by west UP politicians, especially a section of the Jats, with Ajit Singh playing the pivotal role. With the rise of other peasant castes in UP, such as the Yadavs in the post-Charan Singh era, the Jats are placed in a politically disadvantageous position. Being a numerical minority and largely restricted habitat-wise to the western region, the Jats are politically challenged by the numerically dominant Yadavs, inhabiting a larger area of the state. The sheer size of UP is a constraint on the Jats political ascendancy. In the western region, they have a substantial population and occupy a dominant place in the agrarian economy. Thus, they believe that the creation of 'Harit Pradesh' would enable them to dominate the politics of the new state, with one of their leaders becoming the chief minister—which is well nigh impossible in the present political map of UP.

Harit Pradesh

The state of "Uttar Pradesh is essentially an artifact" or "largely a collection of geographic and historical regions" made up of the areas which were brought under the colonial administration by conquering or annexing the kingdoms of the Nawabs of Awadh, the Maratha Chieftains and the Raja of Garhwal over a period of more than quarter of a century (1775 to 1856). These areas were divided into two distinct administrative units—The North West Province (later renamed as the Province of Agra) and Awadh. In 1902 these were brought under the single administration of the Provinces of Agra and Awadh, later rechristened as the United Provinces. The autonomous princely states of Rampur and Tehri Garhwal became constituents of the province in 1949. The name of the province was again changed to Uttar Pradesh ("Northern Province") in January 1950 (See Brass, 1983: 229-231; 1985; 230: UPZAC Report, Vol.I, 1948: 79-80; Kumar, 2000a: 50). In 1950, there were 51 districts in UP. Their number kept increasing and with creation of 15 more districts during the two regimes of Mayawati (between September 1995 and September 1997), their number became 82. The formation of Uttaranchal on November 9, 2000, left UP with 70 districts.

With the exclusion of Uttaranchal, the districts of UP can be categorised into six regions: 1) Rohilkhand, 2) Upper Doab, 3) Lower Doab, 4) Oudh, 5) eastern districts, and 6) Bundelkhand (See Brass, 1985: 71-73). On the basis of their geographical location in the state, the districts can be identified as those belonging to western, central, eastern and southern UP or Bundelkhand region. Such categorisation is relevant for the discussion in this chapter, as it is used in almost all kinds of discourse. There is, however, no such official categorisation.

The recent Harit Pradesh demand specifies the inclusion of 23 districts, they being Agra, Mainpuri, Firozabad, Aligargh, Bareilly, Badaun, Bulandshahr, Etah, Mathura, Meerut, Ghaziabad, Moradabad, Pilibhit, Rampur, Saharanpur, Muzaffarnagar, Bijnor, Hardwar, Shahjahanpur, Mahamaya Nagar, Baghpat, Gautam Budh Nagar and Jyotiba Phule Nagar.[1] These districts mainly belong to Rohilkhand, the Upper and Lower Doab regions. Over the years different names have been given to the proposed state, e.g., Doab Pradesh, Ganna Pradesh, Kisan Pradesh, Jatistan, Brij Pradesh, Pashchimanchal and Harit Pradesh.[2] Harit

1. Hardwar has already been included in the new state of Uttaranchal which was formed on November 9, 2000. The BKU led by Mahendra Singh Tikait has launched an agitation against its inclusion in the new state. But the main political forces that are demanding Harit Pradesh are not participating in this agitation nor has the BKU joined the one for Harit Pradesh. The name of another district, Mahamaya Nagar, has been changed to Hathras in the official records.

2. Though one is not sure as to when the new nomenclature will be repalced by another, for brevity, I have used 'Harit Pradesh' and 'separate state of western Uttar Pradesh' interchangeably throughout this chapter.

Pradesh, meaning Green Province, signifies the agricultural prosperity of the region and is the latest nomenclature given in June 2000. On the eve of the 1996 UP Assembly elections, the Kisan Vikas Party (KVP) was founded by Om Singh Tomar for the creation of a separate state. The KVP contested in several constituencies of Western UP with the separate state demand as the main issue on its agenda. But the party performed badly in the election and ceased to exist. Nevertheless, the demand continues to be raised by certain political parties, individuals, lawyers and organisations. Prominent among these include Ajit Singh with his party which has had different names—the Bharatiya Kisan Kamgar Party (BKKP), the Rashtriya Lok Dal (RLD), the Paschimi Uttar Pradesh Rajya Nirman Morcha (PUPRNM, Western Uttar Pradesh State Formation Front) and Harit Pradesh Nirman Samiti (HPNS). The PUPRNM was set up in 1997 following a seminar held in the Mavalankar Hall, New Delhi, at the initiative of Ajit Singh. It aimed at mobilising public opinion in favour of a separate state of western UP (Interview, July 9, 1999, Gyanendra Sharma, president youth wing of the PUPRNM). With the renaming of the proposed state as Harit Pradesh, HPNS was formed on June 27, 2000 at a meeting of leaders from western UP held in New Delhi (*Hindustan Times*, June 28, 2000).

After losing the 1996 Lok Sabha election to the BJP, Ajit Singh has kept himself busy raising the statehood demand.[3] On September 23, 1998, eight MLAs belonging to the BKKP led by Kokab Hamid walked out of the UP Vidhan Sabha when their demand was not met during the presentation of Uttar Pradesh Reorganisation Bill, 1998 by Kalyan Singh Government for a separate state of Uttaranchal. The bill was passed with some amendments to the original bill.[4] Again on October 24, 2000, Kokab Hamid, now from the

3. Advocates of Harit Pradesh suggest that, apart from the newly created state of Uttaranchal, the existing state of Uttar Pradesh should be divided into four states, i.e., (1) Harit Pradesh; (2) Poorvanchal, consisting the 27 districts of Mau, Allahabad, Kaushambi, Ajamgarh, Ballia, Behraich, Balrampur, Gonda, Shravasti, Siddarthnagar, Basti, Maharajgang, Deoria, Khushinagar, Ghazipur, Jaunpur, Sultanpur, Kabir Nagar, Pratapgarh, Sonbhadra, Sant Ravidas Nagar, Mirzapur, Varanasi, Chandauli, Faizabad, Ambedkar Nagar and Gorakhpur; (3) Bundelkhand consisting the seven districts of Jhansi, Banda, Jalaun, Shahujinagar, Lalitpur, Hamirpur, Mohaba and should include the Madhya Pradesh districts of Sagar, Damoh, Datia, Bhind, Murena, Narsinghgarh, Panna, Chatarpur; and (4) 14 Madhya Pradesh/Awadh Pradesh/ Madhyanchal comprising Lucknow, Barabanki, Hardoi, Unnao, Sitapur, Rae Bareli, Kheri, Kanpur Nagar, Akbarpur, Fatehpur, Farrukhabad, Etawa, Orraia and Kannauj. (Tomar, n.d.).

4. In fact, on September 18, 1998, the opening day of the Assembly session, some ministers belonging to the BJP also demanded that a separate state consisting of 12 districts of eastern UP should be created. They shouted "No Uttaranchal without Poorvanchal". The demand, however, was dropped at the instance of the then Chief Minister Kalyan Singh (*The Times of India*, September 19, 2000).

platform of the Rashtriya Lok Dal (aka BKKP) introduced a resolution on the floor of the Legislative Assembly for the division of the UP into four states including the Harit Pradesh. The resolution was, of course, defeated.[5] During the past five years the BKKP/RLD modus operandi for mobilising the public opinion has included public meetings, *padyatras*, press conferences, press statements, *jan andolan* (mass movement), announcement to start agitation, holding of seminars and brainstorming sessions.[6] But none of these has been effective enough to mobilise the masses. Even threats of agitations have been confined to press statements. For example, Ajit Singh had promised that he would make the issue of statehood issue a plank in the Lok Sabha election of 1998. But nothing of this sort happened. However, he seems to have been working more systematically since 2000, with an eye on the UP elections to be held in 2002. In his public meetings and statements he has made it clear that the issue would be the main plank of his party.

The veracity of Ajit Singh's statements, attempts to forge alliances with other parties and mobilise people through the *padyatras*, etc., is subject to the outcome of the election to be held in 2002. Whatever the results may be, it is necessary to analyse the other related issues. Who are raising this demand and how strong is the support? What is the regional, caste and political scenario? What impact is it going to have on the electoral politics? This chapter attempts to seek answers to these questions.

---

5. The resolution named three other states to be created as Poorvanchal, Awadh Pradesh (Madhyanchal) and Bundelkhand. It was supported by RLD, left parties, Bahujan Samaj Party, the Rastriya Kranti Party (RKP), Janata Dal and Lok Dal. The Samajwadi Party opposed the resolution; its representative Ambika Chaudhary argued against the resolution on two grounds: one, the move for smaller states was initiated by the RSS and two, the smaller states would never be viable economically (*The Hindu*, October 25, 2000).

6. For examples, see *The Times of India*, March 7, 1998, *Hindustan Times*, October 17, 1998 and November 10, 1998. The invitees to the brainstorming sessions included those leaders from other regions who support the agitation for the formation of small states. The first brainstorming session held in Mavalankar hall, New Delhi, in 1997 was attended among others by the JMM leader Shibhu Soren (Interview: July 9, 1999, Gyanendra Sharma; see also *The Hindu*, August 20, 2000). The second brainstorming session was held on July 16, 2000 in Muzaffarnagar; Prakash Ambedkar, leader of the Bahujan Republican Paksh-Bahujan Mahasangh (BRP-BMS), was one of the participants in this meeting (see *The Hindu*, July 17, 2000; *The Times of India*, July 17, 2000).

   The PUPRNM also organised sit-ins at the district headquarters in the first week of August 1998. The agitation had turned violent; students courted arrest around 70-80 of them were sent to jail. (Interview July 9, 1999; Gyanendra Sharma, president Youth wing of the PUPRNM). These activities of the advocates of Harit Pradesh are reminiscent of how the leaders of Haryana participated in various conferences and meetings, and submitted memoranda to urge upon the government to create a Haryana Prant before and after its creation (see Kumar, 1991: 123-124).

History of the Demand

Though the demand for a separate state was voiced earlier, it became a regular affair only in the late 1990s. Highlighting the cultural links between the Hindu Jats of Haryana and Bharatpur in 1931, Chaudhary Lalchand, president of the Delhi session of Jat Mahasabha demanded a separate state for 'Hindu Jats' comprising Meerut, Agra and Delhi divisions. In 1935, Chhotu Ram demanded a province populated by Hindu Jats alone, including south-east Punjab (now Haryana), western UP and Rajasthan, so as to protect the cultural and economic interests of the Hindu Jats (Datta, 1999: 134). In 1954 as well, 97 MLAs hailing from western UP gave a signed memorandum to the Central Commission for the Reorganistion of the States demanding a separate state for western UP districts and some parts of Haryana. The demand was based on cultural and linguistic affinities, historical precedent and administrative convenience (Brass, 1974: 18). The Janata Party MLA, Sohanveer Singh Tomar (convenor of the PUPRNM) raised it in the UP Assembly in the 1970s. Even Charan Singh had preferred smaller states to bigger ones like UP and Bihar. He argued that these states were difficult to manage from the administrative point of view. He said, "remarkable progress made by smaller states may provide clue to how states can be reorganised." (*Hindustan Times*, October 30, 1979).

Why a Separate State?

The convenor of the PUPRNM, Sohanveer Singh Tomar has explained the reasons for the need to create the separate state in a booklet *Uttar Pradesh Ka Punargathan Kyon?* (Why Reorganisation of UP?). In a message through the booklet, Ajit Singh pointed out the following facts: the main reason for the chronic maladministration and lack of development in UP was that one single administrative jurisdiction covered the whole vast state; democracy usually succeeds in "small units"; bigger the units, lesser contact with the masses; UP is the biggest state in the country and no unit in any democratic system in the world is so big from the demographic point of view; it is not possible for one "centre" like Lucknow to provide efficient administration to the far-flung corners of the state; it is humanly not possible for the chief minister to tour all districts even once; the headquarters of the judiciary, public service commission, etc., are about 300-600 kms away from many regions; it means that the constitutional and administrative institutions are beyond the reach of people in a large part of the state (Tomar, n.d.).[7] In support of his

7. *Hindustan Times*, March 12, 2000 also mentions the distance between various district headquarters and Allahabad.

arguments Ajit Singh often refers to Dr. B.R. Ambedkar.[8] The views of Ajit Singh, which he reiterates in all his public statements are shared by a large section of people in Meerut and Muzaffarnagar districts.[9] They provide the following arguments:

1. The government in Lucknow has neglected the western region: (a) its development is insignificant in comparison to its contribution to the state; *Paschimi Uttar Pradesh Ki Kamai Ko Poorvi Uttar Pradesh Walein Khatein Hein* (western UP toils and eastern UP eats) is the common refrain in the region; other parts of UP are developing at the cost of this region. Ajit Singh has said that the region contributes 70 per cent of the entire state's income but not even 20 per cent of it flows back to the region. (*Amar Ujala,* July 19, 1998); (b) western UP has made a powerful contribution to the defence and security of the country in the form of the Jat Regiment which has been at the forefront of the country's defence.
2. Both the capital Lucknow, which dominates the state's politics and is the administrative headquarters and Allahabad, the judiciary headquarters with its High Court, are too far from western UP; visiting these cities is too expensive and time consuming. Whenever people of western UP visit Allahabad High Court or Lucknow, they are cheated, discriminated against and looked down upon by the locals. Experts in various selection committees for government jobs belong to the east and discriminate against the candidates from the west.
3. Economic and educational discrimination: Most of the factories are located in eastern UP. The academic institutions of western UP are given much less grant-in-aid than to those of eastern and central UP.
4. Too unwieldy to govern: Due to huge population, number of districts, different agro-climatic and cultural zones, UP is too unwieldy for good governance. The states like Haryana and Punjab have made progress due to their smaller size.

---

8. Ambedkar favoured smaller states. Recommending the break up of the north Indian states of UP, Bihar and Madhya Pradesh, he suggested the division of Uttar Pradesh into three states, e.g., Western Uttar Pradesh, Central Uttar Pradesh and Eastern Uttar Pradesh and Meerut, Cawnpore and Allahabad as their capitals respectively. The Western UP in the scheme of Ambedkar consisted the areas of the newly constituted Uttaranchal as well (see Ambedkar, 1989: 150-151).
9. It is based on the discussions which I held with groups of people in Meerut and Muzaffarnagar; Personal interview Gyanendra Sharma, July 9, 1999 and newspaper reports.

5. Political discrimination: The politicians from the eastern side attempt to keep those from the western side out of important political positions. To substantiate this point, the president of the youth wing of the PUPRNM, Gyanendra Sharma said that from 1992 to 1997 the state government had banned elections to the student unions in the west, though it was allowed in the east. He also said that most of the chief ministers hailed from eastern UP and they took decisions in favour of their regions (Interview; July 9, 1999). Echoing simlar views, Ajit Singh alleged, "though they (Mayawati, Kalyan Singh and Mulayam Singh Yadav) all hail from Western UP, once they reach Lucknow they forget about this place because eastern and central UP are where votes are concentrated" (*The Times of India*, March 1998).
6. Cultural differences: The central and eastern parts share a common culture with western Bihar rather than with western UP. Besides, the western UP has a legacy of distinct historical significance. Lord Krishna was born in Mathura, the capital of Pandavas was Hastinapur and the first war of Indepedence in 1857 was fought in Meerut—all located in the western region.

Some of these arguments/perceptions seem to be real and others constructed. For example, the one relating to the distance between the state capital Lucknow and the centre of legal machinary Allahabad are based on the genuine grievances of the residents of western UP. Whether they are real or perceived they are relevant as long as they help mobilise support.

The Demands

In the light of the above arguments and preceptions, the following demands have been raised from time to time:

i. A branch of mini secretariat be set up in western UP;
ii. An agricultural university should be set up in the west and Meerut college, being the biggest college in the state, be declared a university;
iii. A bench of Allahabad High Court be set up on the western side; and
iv. The separate state issue came as the final and the ultimate demand. It must be noted that before the demand was taken up more vigorously, the west wing's political elite concentrated on the other three less extreme demands. When these were not conceded, they were convinced that the only solution to the problems would be either to leave the

people of this region to themselves or create the state of Harit Pradesh. It is noteworthy that the demand for separate state was preceded by the lawyers' agitation for the establishment of a separate bench of Allahabad High Court in western UP. Their failure paved the way for some politicians to raise the issue of the separate state more forcefully. The following section discusses the lawyers' agitation.

The Lawyers' Agitation[10]

For almost two decades the lawyers of western UP have been agitating for the establishment of a bench of Allahabad High Court in Meerut.[11] The lawyers had set up the Paschimi Uttar Pradesh Bench Sangharsh Samiti (PUPBSS) and the demand was raised as far back as in the 1950s. But it was from the 1970s that almost every year the lawyers have been agitating on this issue. They have taken recourse to demonstrations, rallies in Meerut or Delhi, launched Jail Bharo Andolan (court arrest movement). They have presented memoranda and charter of demands to the Prime Minister, UP Chief Minister, the District Magistrate of Meerut and the Speaker of the Lok Sabha. The longest agitation of the lawyers took place in 1981. Since then the lawyers observe strike on every Saturday.

Arguments in Favour of the High Court Bench[12]

Apart from the arguments given for a separate state, such as the long distance between the western districts and Allahabad, the following arguments are also made specially regarding the need for a separate bench of the High Court in a western district:

1. The seats of the (new) High Court at Allahabad and its bench at Lucknow, which were created according to the High Court (Amalgamation) Order,

---

10. The discussion on the lawyers' agitation is based on the interviews held in the month of September 1998 with Chandra Shekher Sharma, advocate Meerut district court; Som Datt Tyagi, Secretary Meerut Bar Association, 1978; and on the relevant reports from the newspapers (1983–1999): *Hindustan Times, Amar Ujala, Dainik Jagran,The Indian Express, Punjab Kesari, The Times of India, Hindustan, Janata Express, Meerut Samachar* and *Dainik Prabhat*.

11. Before their inclusion in the new state of Uttaranchal, the lawyers belonging to UP hill districts like Dehradun, Pauri, Nainital, which was then part of UP, also participated in the agitation for a bench of the High Court. In fact, establishment of a High Court at Nainital had provoked lawyers from Dehradun to agitate for having it shifted to their town. Following western UP lawyers suit, those of Dehradun have decided to observe strike on every Saturday (see *The Hindu*, November 1, 2000).

12. Based on the memorandum/charter of demands of the High Court Bench Sthapana Sangharsh Samiti, interviews and newspapers.

1948 are not permanent.[13] The location of these seats can be changed in accordance with the provisions of the Order; the High Court or division benches would be set up at Allahabad or at such other places, as chosen by the Chief Justice with the approval of the UP governor.[14] This implies the situation (the long distances to Allahabad and Lucknow, etc.), demands that there be a separate bench of the Allahabad High Court in western UP. It will be in consonance with the provisions of the Order of 1948. Hence, the demand for the bench is legal. This argument is given to refute the resolution of the Allahabad Bar Association, which termed the demand as unconstitutional (see Premi, 1985).

2. From the point of view of the population, the case of UP is fit for setting up the bench in western UP. The state, with the population of 15 crore, has only one bench of the Allahabad High Court—and that at Lucknow. But states which are much smaller, even those with one-third of UP's population have at least two benches of the High Court. West UP, whose population is around 4.5 crore, does not have any bench while the states with lesser population like Rajasthan have it. Even smaller states have benches of the High Courts. For example, Guwahati High Court has its benches in Imphal, Kohima and Shillong.
3. Western UP is discriminated against, even if the regional proportions of the state's area are taken into consideration for the setting up of a court. The districts that are agitating for a bench cover 33.61 per cent (98,933 sq.kms) area whereas the total area of UP is 2,94,413 sq. kms. And yet, the Allahabad region, covering 107,400 sq.kms., has the High Court (HC) and Lucknow (central region), slightly more than 62,000 kms., has a bench.
4. The number of pending cases in the High Court are piling up and a large number of them are cases from the west. Pursuing a case is a time and money consuming exercise for the western citizens. The clients will continue to face problems till a bench of Allahabad High Court is set up further west. Within two months (November 1, 1996 to December 31, 1997), the number of pending cases at the Allahabad High Court increased by 19,658, while within the same period only 421 cases were resolved. Till December 31, 1997, there were 5,23,853 pending cases in

13. The (new) High Court at Allahabad came into existence as a result of the amalgamation of the old High Court at Allahabad and Oudh Chief Commissioner's Court at Lucknow.

14. The High Court Bench Sthapana Sangharsh Samiti Paschimi Uttar Pradesh, Memorandum/ Charter of demands.

Allahabad High Court. Of these 49 per cent belonged to west UP. The number can be speedily slashed down if there was a HC bench in the west.

5. The lawyers complain that the government and politicians are not bothered about their problems. They give priority to the issues that help them in their power game. For example, 21 new districts have been created in UP, of which 8 are in western UP. The logic behind the creation of the new districts should also apply for creation of a High Court bench.

Initially, the agitation started in Meerut in 1978. In the following period it was extended to other areas to dispel the impression that it was a demand of the lawyers of Meerut region only. (Inteview: Som Datt Tyagi, Sectretary Bar Association; September 10, 1978). Although the lawyers of 16 districts of western UP—Meerut, Ghaziabad, Bulandshahr, Mathura, Saharanpur, Moradabad, Agra, Rampur and some hill districts like Dehradun, Pauri and Nainital have supported the agitation, those from Meerut division have played the most active role. In 1983 the agitation resulted in a scuffle between the police and the lawyers. On their way to present a memorandum to the President of India, the lawyers violated the prohibitory orders leading to a police lathi-charge. Around 71 lawyers were arrested (*The Indian Express*, December 8, 1983; *Meerut Samachar,* December 10, 1983; *The Times of India*, December 8, 1983).

The agitation lacked popular support, though the more knowledgeable section of the society sympathised with it. Besides, after the submission of Jaswant Singh Commission Report (discussed in the next para), the lawyers of Agra and Bareilly region became indifferent, and after the passage of resolution for Uttarakhand the lawyers from Dehradun, Nainital and Pauri lost interest in the agitation. It evoked opposition from the lawyers of Allahabad region.

Jaswant Singh Commission Report

In response to the lawyers' agitation the Central government appointed a commission under the chairmanship of Justice Jaswant Singh on September 24, 1981 to look into the issue.[15] The terms of reference of the Commission were not confined to UP only; it was to consider other demands for the

15. The following discussion is based on the charter of demands of The High Court Bench Sthapana Sangharsh Samiti, Paschimi Uttar Pradesh; Meerut Bar Association.

establishment of separate benches wherever they were made in the country and submit the report within six months of its commencement. But several six monthly extensions were given and the report was submitted four years later, on April 30, 1985.

The Commission recommended the setting up of the bench in western UP but in Agra, not Meerut. It also recommended setting up of circuit bench in Dehradun and Nainital. This invited the wrath of the Meerut lawyers. They had been opposed to the appointment of the Commission right from the start, as they felt it was an imposition on them and had accepted it very reluctantly. As for the recommendations, they said it was a ploy to divide the lawyers.

With the submission of the Jaswant Singh Report, the focus of the lawyers' agitation shifted to its implementation. The report became a bone of contention between the Central and state governments. The former referred the report to the state government for its opinion. The BJP (Atal Bihari Vajpayee) criticised the Centre for delaying the implementation of the report by referring it to the state government. Union Law Minister H.R. Bharadwaj accused the BJP and the Janata Party of instigating the lawyers of Allahabad against setting up of the HC bench in western UP. The state referred the matter back to the Centre. Politicians in Allahabad too found it politically expedient to lend their support. While Allahabad's MP, Amitabh Bachchan opposed the creation of the bench, Hemvati Nandan Bahuguna showed indifference.[16] Mayawati decided to set up the bench at Meerut during her chief ministership but withdrew it within a couple of days due to the opposition from Allahabad region. Similarly, Kalyan Singh of the BJP, when he was the chief minister avoided the issue by referring the issue to the Chief Justice of the Allahabad High Court who rejected the bench demand (*Hindustan Times*, May 31, 1998).

Issues Combined

In the whole politicking over the report, the bench and the state issues got linked. Against the background of failed lawyers' agitation, lack of popular support, politicians' ambivalence and the Meerut's lawyers' opposition to the Jaswant Report's choice of Agra as the site for the bench, the lawyers and politicians of the Meerut region came to realise that the only solution to the problems was to separate from UP. Now, their demand was not a bench, but a

16. In reaction to Amitabh Bachchan's stance on the issue, the lawyers of Meerut had appealed to the cinema owners of the district not to screen his films.

High Court in a new state. It would also unite the districts, specially Meerut and Agra.[17] However, the the bench agitation again gained momentum in the form of rallies and meetings in February and March 2000 and the Saturday boycott, started in 1891 which still continues (See *Hindustan Times*, March 12, 2000).

Mobilisation of Various Groups

Ajit Singh has attempted to mobilise various groups, e.g., political parties, students, lawyers, the trading community and the chambers of commerce to support the Harit Pradesh call.[18] Attitudes of the major political parties and leaders have been dictated by political considerations. While a section of the BJP leadership is not averse to the idea of the division of UP even after the creation of Uttaranchal and the Congress has not taken a categorical stand on it, the SP is opposed to it.[19] As mentioned earlier, the SP along with the BJP opposed the RLD's resolution in the UP Assembly proposing the division of UP into four more states. Contradicting the RLD, they said that smaller states are not economically viable. The BSP, the Rashtriya Kranti Party, the Janata Dal, the Lok Dal supported the resolution of the RLD. At a meeting organised by Ajit Singh in Lucknow, even the former Prime Minister H.D. Deve Gowda, along with the representatives of the BSP expressed support for the creation of a separate state, such as Harit Pradesh (*The Hindu*, October 19, 2000).[20]

---

17. Ajit Singh links the demand for separate state with unwillingness of the other politicians to set a separate bench of the Allahabad High Court (*Amar Ujala,* July 18, 1988). It is noteworthy that other politicians were sore over the suggestion to set up bench at Agra but Ajit Singh chose to keep out of this new development because as a state leader he could not show a bias in district level rivalries.

18. Or mobilisation of lawyers, students, trading community and chambers of commerce (see *Dainik Jagran* June 24, 2000; *Hindustan Times,* November 13, 2000).

19. There are differences within the BJP on the issue of creation of smaller states. The president of the party Bangaru Laxman supports the idea of small states. L.K. Advani said that the NDA Government would also support it if the concerned state Legislature passes a resolution to that effect. Chief Minister Ram Prakash Gupta (BJP) opposed any further divisions after the creation of Uttaranchal. The president of the Uttar Pradesh BJP unit Kalraj Mishra agreed with the need for creation of Harit Pradesh but pointed out that time for it was not favourable as the state of Uttaranchal had just been created. Another BJP leader from western UP, Bireshwar Tyagi, rejected the idea as politically motivated while some other BJP leaders from the region supported the demand for a separate state of western UP (see *The Times of India*, October 1, 1998; *Dainik Jagran*, June 24, 2000; *Hindustan Times*, December 24, 2000). As mentioned earlier, on September 18, 1998, some members belonging to the BJP had walked out of the UP Assembly demanding the creation of separate state of "Poorvanchal".

20. Tbe BSP activists in a group discussion in which I was present on November 18, 2000 in Meerut expressed the need for a separate state of western UP and said they would like to support an agitation, if asked by their party. But they also pointed out that at present the demand is being raised by Jats, because the latter are facing political crisis. Instead of Jats taking lead in such an agitation, they would like a Dalit party to do so.

As mentioned earlier, Ajit Singh declared that he would make the issue of Harit Pradesh a plank in the 2002 Assembly elections. He said it was essential to get at least 50 out of 100 MLAs elected on a single platform in order to be an effective force in the formation of the government;[21] this would also help in the passage of a Harit Pradesh resolution in the Assembly. In his assessment, no party would get the necessary majority for the formation of the government in the state. He appealed to the electorate to vote for those parties which would support this issue, adding that his party would ally with any pro-Harit Pradesh party. He hoped that once the momentum for the formation of the state picked up, other parties like the BSP, the NCP and SP would also support the issue (*Hindustan Times*, October 11, 2000).[22] Keeping this in view, Ajit Singh has entered into an alliance with Prakash Ambedkar and is hobnobbing with the NCP so as to be able to bargain on the issue with whoever becomes the chief minister.

Ajit Singh, strident in his attitude towards the SP, has accused Mulayam Singh Yadav of having backtracked on the issue because he, along with Charan Singh, was one of the signatories to a document demanding a separate state. Ajit Singh accused the opponents of the small states as those disregarding the views of Dr. B.R. Ambedkar.[23]

Significance of the issue can be gauged from certain decisions of the then BJP-led government in UP on issues related to the demand. Since the Lok Dal had decided to make it the main plank in the 2002 elections, the BJP was not going to let the issue slip out of its hands. While the BJP leadership at the state level seemed to oppose the demand, those in the region were supporting it. The state government's choice of Meerut as the third centre for conducting Provincial Services Examination, (the other two being Lucknow and Allahabad) and its sanctioning of a proposal to set up an Agriculture University in Meerut by converting the western campus of the Gobind Ballabh Pant University situated at Modipuram into a separate university are attempts to meeting the

---

21. Addressing a rally of his supporters at Shamli on Novemer 9, 1998, Ajit Singh said: "The moment we have enough MPs and MLAs with us, a separate state will become a reality" (*Hindustan Times*, November 10, 1998).

22. BSP's support for small states is confirmed from the stance which its MLAs took in the Rajasthan assembly recently. BSP MLAs, led by Mahir Azad, along with the Independent MLAs demanded creation of a separate state for the eastern districts of Rajasthan—Bharatpur, Alwar, Dholpur, Sawai Madhupur, Dausa and Karauli. They alleged the politicians and planners belonging to the western and southern Rajasthan have discriminated against the east and monopolised the invesments for their regions (*The Hindu*, November 3, 2000).

23. See fn. 8.

demands raised by the proponents of Harit Pradesh (*Hindustan Times*, August 19, 2000).

Caste and the Demand for Harit Pradesh

While the lawyers of all castes are pressing for a HC bench in Meerut, it is mainly the Jats who are spearheading the separate state movement. The Jats now want a political domain in the form of a state, not just a political domination of the region. In the demise of Charan Singh, who was their source of inspiration, moral strength and caste solidarity, the Jats of this region had lost a leader of national stature who enjoyed mass following throughout UP. The post-Charan Singh era has also witnessed the rise of a generation of ambitious politicians among the Jats, just as in other communities. The caste map of a state as big as UP clearly shows that its size is the main impediment to the fulfilment of Jat ambitions. But the politicians of the other regions in UP quite naturally think differently and pursue different objectives, in the face of which the Jat influence has declined considerably. Their dominance has been restricted to the western region and this constricting situation will continue as long as it remains a part of UP. Other castes like Yadavs are placed in more advantageous position. The reasons for the Jats' political decline lie in their numerical inferiority to other peasant castes. According to the 1931 census, the Jats formed only 1.6 per cent of the state's population, while Yadavs constituted 8.7 per cent (see Hasan, 1989: Table 2). A survey conducted in 1991 showed the OBCs as forming 37 per cent of voters in UP, of which Yadavs were the largest (see Hasan, 1998: 138). And in 1994, the Panchayati Raj Deparment of the Samajwadi-BSP government conducted a rapid census to assess the population of the OBCs in UP for facilitating reservations in the urban and rural local bodies elections. The results showed that the Jats, along with Bhumihars and Tyagis constituted only 2 per cent of the population, while the OBCs, which included Yadavs constituted 37 per cent (Hasan, 1998: 166 and Table 4.10).[24] In the Assembly elections held between 1952 and 1980, the percentage of the Jat MLAs along with those of Bhumihars and Tyagis varied between 4.49 (in 1969) and 6.95 (in 1974), of Ahirs (Yadavs) MLAs along with those Kurmies, Lodhs and Gujjars between 6 (in 1952) and 23.26 (in 1974) (see Hasan, 1998: Table 4.2).

---

24. In March 2000, the Jats of UP were included in the OBC category.

Politics of Charan Singh

It is pertinent to ask here how the Jat strongman, Charan Singh was able to dominate the state's politics of UP despite being a leader of a numerically handicapped caste. An analysis of his policies and strategy for the upliftment of the backward classes and peasantry and his emergence at a critical moment on the political scene will best explain his rise to a position of power and influence.

1. The policies and strategy: Charan Singh was the undisputed leader of the peasantry and backward classes in the entire UP during the 1950s and 1960s, both when he was in the Congress and after he left the party, right till his death in 1987. Though the backward class peasantry of eastern and central UP usually supported socialist parties, they had supported Charan Singh in his individual capacity even when he was in the Congress Party. As the disintegration of the socialist movement in UP almost coincided with Charan Singh's exit from the Congress, the only option left for them was to support the BKD/BLD, the party of the one man they revered, Charan Singh. He was accepted as a leader by the non-Jat peasants in the eastern and central regions, apart from the Jats in the west. As a Congressman, he had built a Yadav-Kurmi-Koeri base of his own in the east and middle UP. During the 1950s and 1960s he frequently visited these regions, talking to and winning over the backward class peasantry. He pointed out the benefits of the land reforms introduced by the Congress, in which he had played the main role. When he was the Chief Minister, he had consolidated his position as a leader of the backward classes and peasantry. His was accused by UP's high caste Congress leadership of favouring the backward classes at the cost of the high. Charan Singh turned the table on them by accusing them of favouring the high castes (See Singh, 1992: 128-29, 158-59; Hasan, 1989: 175-77; 1998: 131; Brass, 1983: 307-9). His differences within the Congress led to his defection just at the right time to form the BKD in 1969. Contrary to the Congress's policies, he gave representation to the middle castes and backward classes, e.g., Ahirs, Yadavs, Kurmis, etc., in the allotment of tickets during his reign and as the head of his party at the district and state levels (See Hasan 1998: 131-132; 1989: 191; Johnson, 1975: 242-65 and Shrivastava, 1976: 333-34). He also continued to ally with the backward class leadership

in UP and Bihar like Mulayam Singh Yadav, Ram Naresh Yadav or Karpoori Thakur. Charan Singh remained the undisputed leader of the backward class peasantry in North India till his demise in 1987.

2. The epochal factors: Charan Singh dominated the politics of backward classes and peasantry of UP in a particular phase of peasant politics, that is, when there was no leader in the state from any other peasant community who could match his stature. It was his unrivalled leadership and his highly effective policies that made him the one and only leader of the downtrodden section of the peasantry which also formed the majority caste grouping of Yadavs, Kurmis, Koeris, Lodhs, etc.

During the three decades after Independence, there also emerged a new generation of leadership among the non-Jat peasant castes like Yadavs. They were the main beneficiaries of the fruits of land reforms—mainly the abolition of landlordism—and the Green Revolution. The vacuum created by Charan Singh's death was filled up by the leaders belonging to the non-Jat peasant castes, mainly Yadavs. Leadership of Tikait suffered from caste dissensions and "hyper-localism" (See Singh, 1992: 97-103). The epochal factors now favour Yadavs more than the Jats. As mentioned earlier, they are better placed from the point of view of caste population and its regional spread.

Conclusion

The agitation for Harit Pradesh is still in its callow youth, as it were. It has passed through two phases so far. The first was supported almost only by a section of the Jats. The second phase has seen the involvement of other communities and social groups like the students, lawyers, chamber of commerce and traders as well. But the mobilisation is still confined to the leadership of various groups and communities and the masses are not involved. However, the people in the west, cutting across socio-economic backgrounds want a separate state, as it would bring the instrument of justice and the machinery of administration not only within their reach but also within their domain. They would be freed of their dependence on the distant cities of Lucknow and Allahabad, from which they have felt estranged for a long time. Job opportunities for all sections of the society would increase manifold. Besides, the apprehensions of the other castes about Jat domination has been allayed by the realisation that, in electoral politics, no single community can prevail on its own. It has to take support of others as well.

Be that as it may, the agitation is now afflicted by conflicts among the Jats themselves. Some of the Jat leaders who were initially involved in the agitation are no longer active. Besides, the chief of the BKU, Mahendra Singh Tikait, has not joined the agitation. Instead, he has launched an agitation (September and October 2000) for retrieving Hardwar and Udham Singh Nagar from Uttaranchal.

Except issuing statements, holding press conferences and rallies, etc., the advocates of Harit Pradesh have not exploited the potential of the masses for support to the agitation. At present, it is an issue raised by the leadership who want their political accommodation. The agitation for Harit Pradesh has the potential of developing into the assertion even of nationality, if the realisation of the people for a separate state of western UP is exploited. But it seems that the leadership of the agitation does not accord priority to the mobilisation of peoples' support beyond their participation in the election. Its main focus is on getting an adequate number of MLAs from pro-separation parties elected.

The Harit Pradesh issue has potential implications for the 2002 UP Assembly elections. In a bid to get an adequate number of MLAs, which would enable him to get the separate state resolution passed in the Legislative Assembly, RLD president Ajit Singh has kept alliance options open. Except for the opposition from Mulayam Singh Yadav's SP and the Congress's indifference, the major parties in UP like BJP, BSP and the RKP are, in principle, not opposed to 'Harit Pradesh'. Its impact on the election will depend on how effective a plank the RLD or any other political force will make out of the issue. It might lead to polarisation of the supporters and opponents. There is a possibility of the BJP trying to outbid the RLD in demanding a state, as it did by declaring the Jats as OBCs in March 2000.

I am thankful to Prof. C.P. Bhambhri, Prof. A.R. Khan and Dr. R.K. Barik for their suggestions and comments on the drafts of this chapter.

References

Ambedkar, B.R. (1989). *Dr. Babasaheb Ambedkar Writings and Speeches.* Vol.1. Education Department, Government of Maharastra.

Brass, Paul R. (1983). *Caste, Faction and Party in Indian Politics: Faction and Party.* Vol.1. Delhi: Chanakya Publications.

————. (1984). *Language, Religion and Politics in North India.* Cambridge: Cambridge University Press.

————. (1985). *Caste, Faction and Party in Indian Politics: Election Studies.* Vol.II. New Delhi: Chanakya Publications.

Datta, Nonica (1999). *Forming an Identity: A Social History of the Jats.* New Delhi: Oxford University Press.

Hasan, Zoya (1998). *Quest for Power: Oppositional Movements and Post Congress Politics in Uttar Pradesh.* Delhi: Oxford University Press.

————. (1989). "Power and Mobilisation: Patterns of Resilience and Change Uttar Pradesh Politics", in Frankel R. Francine and M.S.R. Rao (eds.), *Dominance and State Power in Modern India: Decline of the Social Order.* Delhi: Oxford University Press.

Kumar, Pradeep (1991). "Sub-Nationalism in Indian Politics: Formation of a Haryanvi Identity", *Indian Journal of Political Science,* January-March.

————. (2000a). *The Uttaranchal Movement: Construction of a Regional Identity.* New Delhi: Kanishka Publishers.

————. (2000b). "Demand for New States: Cultural Identity Loses Ground to Urge for Development (Commentary)", *Economic and Political Weekly* XXXV(35-36), August 26-September 2.

Memorandum/*Samiti Pashimi Uttar Pradesh.* Memorandum/Charter of demands of the High Charter of demands of the Court Bench. *Sangharsh Samiti Pashimi Uttar Pradesh.*

Premi, Dharamveer (1985). *"Khandpeeth ki Sthapana kya Samvidhan Virodi Hai?", Hindustan,* May 28.

Report of the United Provinces Zamindari Abolition Committee (UPZAC Report). Vol. I. 1948. UP. Allahabad: Superintendent Printing and Stationary.

Singh, Jagpal (1992). *Capitalism and Dependence: Agrarian Politics in Western Uttar Pradesh 1951-1991.* Delhi: Manohar.

Tomar, Sohan Veer Singh (n.d.) *Uttar Pradesh Ka Punargathan Kyon?.* Meerut: Nutan Press.

15 Regionalism in Uttar Pradesh

A Case for Reorganisation of the State

M.P. Dube

Regionalism is an ambiguous and a much debated concept in political science. It defies precision in its definition. The term 'regionalism' represents "the regional idea in action as an ideology, as a special movement, or as the theoretical basis for regional planning : it is also applied to the scientific task of delimiting and analysing regions as entities lacking formal boundaries—."[1] People living in a particular region over a period of time develop an identity affiliation with it. This affiliation is generally the result of special and temporal factors. Religion, language, ethnicity, a common past rooted in history and a common desire to live together in the future are dependent variables that are conducive to the creation of common identity. Any offence against the identity and self-image results reactively in socio-political movements. In this way, regionalism is a geographical term for socio-political movements which seek: (a) to foster or protect an indigenous culture in particular regions, or (b) to decentralise Central governments to an intermediate level between that of the state and the traditional units of local governments. Thus, regionalism involves the delegation of substantial political and legal powers to regional authorities that would be less than sovereignty but more than mere administrative functions. R.A. Seligman and Johnson equate regionalism with "a counter movement to any exaggerated or oppressive form of centralisation."[2] Jyotindra Das Gupta identified it with a "search for an intermediate control system between the centre and periphery for competitive advantage in national arena."[3]

Regionalism is often confused with regionalisation, though their meanings are entirely different. Firstly, regionalism refers to the practice of redistributing certain government powers to territorial authorities, which is an intermediate position in the sharing of power between the Central and

1. Vance, Rupport B. (1968). *Encyclopaedia of Social Sciences* 13: 378.
2. Ibid.: 208-9.
3. Berkley (1970). *Language Conflict and National Development.* p. 17.

local authorities; regionalisation refers to the processes by which central political and administrative authorities have responded to regionalist demands. Secondly, regionalism is a matter of politics whereas regionalisation is a matter of policies. The former starts from the periphery and the latter is the Centre's response.

Regionalism in India

As in Italy and Germany, India's national unification laid the basis of regionalism—a trend accentuated by the increasing importance of economic differentials. The vast landmass of this country, with its multifaceted diversity is comparable only to former Soviet Union, China and Indonesia. But among these pluralist states, India has been the only democracy. A democratic system provides a favourable climate for the growth of regionalism, which in turn creates tension in the body politic and hence is a potential threat to the integrity of the nation. In India, movements based on regional identities have manifested themselves in various forms. There have been agitations for the recognition of their vernaculars, as also movements of backward mass groups to break away from the advanced nation and become a nation themselves. A particular nationality group which was separated from the parent nationality and was living amidst a different cultural group—as a result of administrative unitisation—have launched a movement to rejoin their cultural mainstream and there are movements by groups which were still at a tribal stage of development and wanted a province of their own to minimise exploitation and encroachment[7] by outsiders and lastly, the movement of a group which, though not backward, struggled against centralised policies that were not in the interest of the majority of the people of the area.

Nationalist leaders in India view regionalism as a very serious threat to the unity, peace and progress of the country. It has generally been regarded as something that is anti-national, anti-system, anti-federal and against the basic interests of a well integrated and well developed polity.[8] What are the main causes of regionalism? What are the main factors responsible for the demand for a separate state? What are the main components of identity politics? How far has reorganisation of states been able to address the issues that caused identity based movements? These are some of the questions that need to be addressed before making any critical assessment of sub-regionalism in UP.

7. *Economic & Political Weekly*, July 17-24, 1993, p.1522.
8. Reddy and Sharma (1979). *Regionalism in India : A Study of Telangana*. New Delhi. p.3.

Causes of Regionalism

In the post-Independence constituent Assembly, we resolved to constitute India into a strong nation state and made secularism and modernisation its dominant creed, so as to ensure a place of respect for her in the community of world nations. Framers of the Constitution ignored the burden of primordial and parochial baggage on the shoulders of a nation travelling on the path to modernistic civilisation. Their main concern was the unity and integrity of the nation. But with the initiation of the constitutional process, a process of regionalisation along primordial lines also commenced. As A.D. Pant has remarked: "The federal character of the Indian constitution left no alternative but to recognise the territorial identity of the regions. But the over all emphasis in the Constitution is to condition the growth of regional identity. A great number of factors, primarily primordial in nature, were not accorded any recognition by the Constitution."[9] Initially, it seemed that we were building a strong nation state of 'unity in diversity'. Today we are increasingly witnessing disunity in diversity. In certain sections it is considered that the process of modernisation and secularisation is responsible for all the ills of the body politic and that the growth of regionalism is a reaction to this process. A number of reasons for this deterioration have been thrown about, such as: "the nefarious policies of this party or that; the unscrupulous manipulation of tense situations by one politician or another; the continuance of feudal attitudes that are swamping the modern goals sought by the educated elite; the prevalence of gut religious feelings untempered by secularism; gross social and economic inequality; and the lack of time to build a modern state free from age old divisions."[10] Thus, factors that cause and foster regionalism are cultural, economic and political in nature. It would be too very complex and a long exercise to deal with them in detail in this short chapter. However, efforts have been made to deal with some of the principal factors.

Politics of Linguistic Identity

Language is the most important distinction in group identification. Language is an expression of shared life, thought structure and values of a distinctive group. In India, it has been one of the dominant causes of regionalism. Linguistic loyalties has sometimes resulted in riots, loss of lives and valuable property. Linguistic regionalism has various forms.

---

9. Pant, A.D. (1984). "Foreword" in the Akhtar Majeed (ed.) *Regionalism: Developmental Tensions in India*. New Delhi. p.5.

10. *The Times of India*, New Delhi, December 5, 1990.

At the beginning of the 20th century under the British rule, arguments were advanced for the creation of linguistic units on three grounds. Firstly, it would enable the legislatures to conduct their business in the vernacular. Secondly, it would be possible for people who did not know English to participate in public affairs. Thirdly, the process of administration would be simplified. Partition of Bengal in 1905 was also opposed on linguistic basis. The opposition was so stiff that it had to be annulled in 1911. In 1912, the boundaries of Bihar, Orissa and Assam were fixed on linguistic principle. In 1913, the Andhra Mahasabha was founded with a view to press for the creation of Andhra Pradesh as a Telugu-speaking state out of the Madras Presidency. The concept of Gujarati Asmita was developed and a steady movement for the separation of Gujarat from the Marathas as well as a unification movement of the entire Gujarati speaking people was also launched. On the other hand, groups which belonged to a particular nationality but were either cut off from it or were compelled by the administrative authorities to live amidst different cultural group, launched movements for unification with their kinsfolk.[11]

The Congress leaders also felt that the party could be made a mass organisation only when linguistic sentiments of the people were exploited and the regional languages were made the medium of political communication. In the 1920 Nagpur session of the Congress, linguistic reorganisation of the country was accepted in principle. The Nehru Report of 1928 also favoured the formation of linguistic states. The Congress Party in its election manifesto of 1945-46 committed itself to the reorganisation of the states on linguistic basis. But after the elections in which the Congress won with a thumping majority, its leaders, thoroughly shaken by the partition massacre and mayhem, shelved the move fearing further conflicts. Their mind was preoccupied with the integration of states on the basis of consensual diplomacy, in some cases even with coercion. Of the states situated within the geographical boundaries of the Dominion of India, all (numbering 532) save Hyderabad, Kashmir, Bahawalpur, Junagarh and the Baluchistan states (Chitral, Khairpur, Dir, Swat and Amb) had acceded to the Dominion of India by the 15th August 1947, i.e., before the 'appointed day' itself. At that time, the Government of India was faced with two problems with regard to the states after the accession: (1) shaping the Indian states into sizeable or viable administrative units, and (ii) fitting them into the constitutional structure of India.

11. *Economic & Political Weekly*, July 17-24, 1993, p.1524.

These objectives were sought to be achieved by a three-fold process of integration (known as the 'Patel Scheme'). Two hundred and sixteen states were merged with the geographically contiguous provinces and 61 states were converted into centrally administered areas. The third process was the consolidation of groups of states into new units known as union of states. As many as 275 states were thus integrated into 5 unions—Madhya Bharat, Pepsu, Rajasthan, Saurashtra and Travancore-Cochin. The other three states included in part B were—Hyderabad, Jammu and Kashmir and Mysore. At the time of their accession in 1947, the states in Part B had acceded to only on three subjects *viz.*, defence, foreign affairs and communications. Later, seeing the benefits of the union, all the Rajpramukh of the unions as well as the Maharaja of Mysore signed revised instruments of accession by which all these states acceded to the Dominion of India in respect of all matters included in the union and concurrent legislative lists, except only those relating to taxation. Thus, the states in Part B were brought at par with the states in Part A, subject only to the differences embodied in Article 238 and the supervisory powers of the Centre for the transitional 10-year period (Article 371). Special provisions were made only for Kashmir (Article 370) in view of its special position and problems.[12] Though the integration of the states was completed, the growth of regional identity was conditional. Yet strong expressions of sectoral loyalty was visible in certain regions of the country such as Andhra, Karanataka and Maharashtra. Hence on June 17, 1948, Dr. Rajendra Prasad, the President of the Constituent Assembly appointed a linguistic Provinces Commission consisting of four members with S.K. Dar as its Chairman, to report on the formation of the new provisions of Andhra, Karnataka, Kerala and Maharashtra. The commission, while expressing its views against linguistic reorganisation observed:

"The formation of provinces on exclusively or even mainly linguistic considerations is not in the larger interest of the Indian nation and should not be taken in hand...."[13]

"One of the reasons why the Dar Commission came to this conclusion was that the linguistic reorganisation of the states would create fresh minority problems because no linguistic state would have more than 70 to 80 per cent linguistic homogeneity."[14]

12. Basu, D.D. (1987). *Introduction to the Constitution of India*. Prentice Hall India. pp.45-46.

13. Munshi, K.M. *Indian Constitutional Documents* I: 230-31.

14. Ibid.

The report could not satisfy the supporters of the linguistic principle. Consequently JVP Committee (1948) (J.L. Nehru, V. Patel and Pattabhi Sitaramayya) was constituted to examine the possibility of linguistic reorganisation of states. Keeping the challenges faced by the country and the complexity of the issue in view, the committee was of the view that the reorganisation of the states on a linguistic basis should be postponed for the time being.

On 26th January 1950, the Indian union consisted of 9 Part A states, 8 Part B states, 10 Part C states and 1 Part D state. Most of them were linguistically heterogeneous. Article 3 of the Constitution provided for the formation of new states and alteration of areas, boundaries or names of the existing states. Nehru and his cabinet colleagues were not in favour of any hasty decision with regard to reorganisation of the states. But meanwhile, in Andhra region of the composite state of Madras, the creation of Vishal Andhra Movement was launched. One Seetharam undertook a fast unto death but gave it up on the persuasion of Vinoba Bhave. Another person, Potti Sriramulu, went on a determined fast for the bifurcation of Madras state into Madras and Andhra Pradesh. After 58 days of fasting, he died on December 15, 1952. The movement became violent and many persons were killed. Ultimately, on December 19, 1952, the Prime Minister announced the creation of the Andhra State, which came into existence on October 1, 1955. A States Reorganisation Commission was also formed on December 22, 1952. The commission consisted of Justice F. Fazal Ali (Chairman), H.N. Kunzru and Sardar K.M. Panikker. This commission examined 152,250 memoranda, documents, etc., and interviewed about 9000 persons. The commission came to the conclusion that not only the language and culture factors but others such as the preservation and strengthening of the unity and security, financial, economic and administrative aspects and the successful implementation of the Five Year Plans also needed be taken into consideration. It recommended the establishment of Kerala and Karnataka as separate provinces on linguistic grounds and the wishes of the people but Bombay was kept a bilingual area consisting of the Marathi and Gujarati speaking people. The Marathi speaking areas of Hyderabad were to be transferred to Bombay but certain other Marathi speaking areas were to be taken away to form a separate Vidarbha state. Punjab was also kept bilingual. In October 1953, the Delhi Assembly passed a resolution recommending to the Centre that the boundaries of Delhi state be enlarged by including the contiguous districts of Punjab and UP, so that a unit administratively and economically sound was created. As early as in 1954, 97 MLAs hailing from western UP presented a signed memorandum to the Central Commission for the reorganisation of the states, demanding a separate state for Western UP districts and some parts of Punjab (present Haryana). The demand was 'couched in terms of cultural and linguistic affinities, historical precedent and administrative convenience.'[14A] But the demands were rejected by the SRC. However, K.M. Panikker was not in favour of the merger of Himachal Pradesh with Punjab. Instead, he wanted it to be a centrally administered territory. He was also of the view that Agra should be created as a separate state consisting of certain parts of UP, Madhya Bharat and Vindhya Pradesh. Parliament passed the act on the reorganisation of states on the basis of the SRC's report and instead of 16 states and three centrally administered territories, as recommended by the SRC, it created 14 states and 6 union territories. The process of language and territory delimitation, however, continued even after the reforms of 1956. The Marathas in Bombay started an agitation for the bifurcation of Bombay in 1960 and when that agitation became violent, the Centre decided to bifurcate Bombay in to Maharashtra and Gujarat sectors.

The Sikhs in Punjab were most dissatisfied by the SRC report. In order to press their demand for reorganisation of Punjab on linguistic basis, the Akali Dal, under the leadership of Master Tara Singh started an agitation in 1960. But Nehru refused to be moved on this issue. The agitation for Punjabi Suba was revived again in August 1965 under the leadership of Sant Fateh Singh. Under pressure, the Centre was forced to appoint the S. Hukum Singh Committee to look into the matter. The committee recommended the creation of Punjabi Suba and Haryana on March 22, 1966. The Shah Commission was appointed to demarcate the boundaries. The Central government did not accept the recommendation of the committee that Chandigarh should go to Haryana. It decided to keep it as a union territory. On November 1, 1966 Punjab and Haryana came into existence as separate states. But many vital issues like distribution of river water, mutual claims over Chandigarh, Fazilka and Abohar were left unresolved resulting in unending conflicts.

The process of linguistic reorganisation of states did not stop here. When the republic came into existence, the north-east consisted of the state of Assam and the union territories of Manipur and Tripura. About 217 scheduled tribe groups inhabited the region besides the plains people. Their languages and their offshoots were plethora—a Tower of Babel in the making. In 1963, in

14A. Brauss, Paul R. (1974). *Language, Religion and Politics in North India*, Cambridge University Press. p.18.

order to counter the Naga secession demand, a separate state of Nagaland was carved out. In the rest of the areas, the Assamese language groups retained their hegemony and in order to maintain it, they tried to force Assamese norms on the hill tribals. They were made to feel ashamed of their tribal identity and forced to come into the Assamese 'mainstream' in order to find social acceptability. Secondly, non-Assamese regions of the state were consistently neglected in terms of development. Finally, the encroachment by outsiders into the tribal area sparked off a movement in the region. But it was the the language policy of the Assam government (1960) that was the final straw. The hill people resented imposition of the Assamese language and launched agitations for separate states.[15] It resulted in the creation of the states of Meghalaya, Mizoram, Arunanchal Pradesh, Tripura, Manipur, each with different social customs, ethnic origin, language and inheritance. Initially some of them were union territories but by the mid-1980s all of them were granted statehood. It is to be noted that these states were not constituted entirely on the basis of linguistic homogeneity. Together with language, ethnic-cum-economic considerations played a decisive role in the reorganisation of the north-east.

The linguistic organisations created more problems and social tensions than it resolved. It created a new problem of linguistic minorities. "In most of the states the linguistic majority developed a discriminatory attitude, blatant or subtle, against all other linguistic groups within the areas of the state." As a result, in some states linguistic clashes continue to date, the salient ones being the much vaunted 'sons of the soil' movements, such as the "Maharashtra for Maharashtrians" of Shiv Sena and the Lachit Sena's movements against Bengalis and Marwaris in Assam.

The inter-state boundary dispute and water disputes are also the legacies of the linguistic organisation. All the following have become regionally sensitised because of boundary disputes: between Punjab and Haryana on Chandigarh and Fazilka; between Maharashtra and Karnataka on Belgaum; between Karnataka and Kerala on Kasargod; between Assam and Nagaland on Rengma reserved forests in Rangapani area and on some villages in Desoi Valley; between Assam and Meghalaya on Langpih, Hakumari and Jingiram river area of Garo Hills; between Assam and Arunanchal Pradesh on Pasighat subdivision; and between Manipur and Nagaland on Suku village.

---

15. *Economic & Political Weekly*, July 17-24, 1993, p.1526.

Economic Deprivation

An ethnic group's feelings and aspirations are aroused when confronting economic, cultural, educational and occupational domination by another group. Economic grievances are, more often than not, at the root of political protest, movements and agitations. As B.D. Pant has observed, "Regionalism is the response of unequal sharing of the benefits of developmental activity. It is a protest against stabilisation and monopolisation of advantages through policies aiming at institutionalisation of existing stratification system... It may result from a process of cumulative deequalisation in which any nascent inequality is intensified over time through cumulative causation channels."[16] The feeling of economic deprivation and exploitation has led to various movements all over the country. Gorkhas in the Darjeeling hills are up in arms over economic exploitation by the Bengali majority, Bodos have protested against unequal share in the resources of Assam. The people of Ladakh and Jammu feel that the Kashmir valley has always hogged a larger share of the state's budget, Vidarbha populace feels that the region is neglected, the Jharkhandis had been sore that the wealth from their mineral resources did not flow to them and the Uttarakhandis complained that they had been kept in relative backwardness. In most of the cases, economic grievances are articulated by the elites of the region. Paul Brass has identified "elite competition as the basic dynamic which precipitates ethnic conflict under specific conditions." The interplay of the ethnic-regional elite with the national elite is a powerful catalysis to autonomy demands in India.

To meet these demands, most of the time ad hoc decisions are taken. For instance, autonomous Regional Development Councils were set up in Darjeeling, Bodoland and Ladakh and in 2000, the new states of Uttarakhand, Jharkhand and Chhattisgarh were created more on considerations of economic backwardness and discrimination than on linguistic considerations.

A centralised state is a prime necessity for unhindered growth and development of big money bourgeoisie. Javed Alam correctly remarks that the 'pan-Indian' bourgeoisie in India, unlike in Europe, did not need to champion any particular language and hence the Stalinist formulation that the bourgeoisie promotes regionalist, linguistic state movements does not hold for India.[17] The local investors, unable to compete with the big money bourgeoisie, aim to

16. In Akhtar Majeed (ed.), *op.cit*, p.6.

17. *Economic & Political Weekly*, *op.cit*, p.1528.

protect their territory of operation by putting up the political wall of smaller 'linguistic' states round their domain, thus repelling to quite an extent the onslaught of big money. It is also a popular move amongst the local populace, as a new state means new opportunities for the local job seekers, politicians and investors.[18]

National parties in power, specially the Congress, have been a divided house in the states right since Independence. The main causes are: (1) personality conflicts; (2) a compelling desire to hold on to the levers of power; and (3) issues relating to developmental priorities. This factionalism is focused around the activities of the leading personalities. As a result there is a persistent struggle for control over the party organisation by the rival groups. In a democratic system, every one has the right to try and get his share of the cake. But there is never enough for all and the curtain never goes down in the theatre of the absurd. The strength of a leader is his following. To win and expand this following, the leader and his group resort to firing up identity issues based on region, religion or caste. Whenever an important leader fails to get a berth in the establishment, the separate-state demand gets heated up but cools down as soon as he is accommodated.

Sometimes, regionalism grows as an outcome of personalised politics. Huntington formulated a three-step proposition: when social mobilisation outstrips economic development, social frustration will ensue; when social frustration exceeds social mobility opportunities, political participation will increase; when political participation grows faster than political institutionalisation, the result is political instability. Social frustration and political participation have been evidently increasing in UP. Poor governance combined with corruption and deinstitutionalisation has increased social frustration and political participation. The frustation sometimes manifested itself through autonomy demands.

UP is miniature India. The Indian Statutory Commission described the state as "the most typically Indian of all the provinces." It represents a fine synthesis of Hindu and Muslim cultures. Spread over a geographical area of 241 thousand sq kms, it accounts for about 16 per cent of the total population of the country. It is the largest producer of food grains and oilseeds in the country. It leads all the states of India in the production of wheat, maize, barley, gram, sugarcane and potatoes. The state is divided into eastern, western, central

18. Ibid.

and southern (Bundelkhand) regions. The eastern region and Bundelkhand are relatively more backward and poor. The western region has relatively greater prosperity. Its prosperity can be accounted for by the existence, for a long period, of a network of irrigation cannals, more invigorating climate and of late, faster rate of industrialisation. And yet, it continues to be one of the poorest states in the country. The regions differ from each other in dialects and food habits but there is no abrupt change. These regions do not have any distinctive features from the point of view of religion or caste composition, except in western UP, where there is concentration of Jats in some areas. But today the pulls of regionalism are creating too much tension to hold the state together.

The green revolution in Western UP did benefit the resource rich farmers but the poor peasants did not feel even the "trickle down effect", to use a tasteless phrase much in vogue today. On the other hand, though the eastern region gained through some purposeful investment in research, extension, irrigation and marketing infrastructure, it has not succeeded in shedding the baggage of feudal culture and remains prone to floods and drought. The region suffers from inertia, disease and decay. Bundelkhand is less developed in terms of infrastructure and meagre irrigation facilities combined with infertile land have made the condition worse. Politically too, the region is neglected. In a plurality voting system of democracy, generally constituencies and regions represented by Chief Ministers or important leaders attract more attention of the government and get nourished properly. Bundelkhand region is not so lucky on this score. The region was not privileged to have faction leaders like Sampurnanand, Govind Ballabh Pant, Ch. Charan Singh, C.B. Gupta, Kamalapati Tripathi, Mulayam Singh, Kalyan Singh or Mayawati.

Though language has been the main criteria for the reorganisation of states in India, it cannot be a basis for the reorganisation of UP. No doubt, cultural identity, of which language/dialect is the main component, was one of the important factors responsible for the formation of Uttarakhand.

The feeling of relative exploitation and neglect had led to the upsurge in the demand for statehood in Uttarakhand. The region's political economy has distinctive features. It is a land of a snow-capped mountains, high hills, gushing rivers and rich forests. Its culture and social anthropology has a marked dissimilarity with that of the plains. More than 60 per cent of the area is either forests or mountains above the snow line. The cultivable area forms only a small portion of the total area, of which nearly 11 per cent is arable. People of the region have immense fortitude and endurance. They are known for their bravery and courage in the battlefield, their integrity and honesty. Educated people of the region believe that exploitation coupled with underdevelopment had alienated the hill people. The annual budget provisions for the hill region have always been impressive on paper. But despite an investment of over thousands of crores in infrastructure over the past decade, there is little to show by way of development. Even though three of the Chief Ministers, G.B. Pant, H.N. Bahuguna and N.D. Tiwari belonged to this region and the region sent to the Union Council of Ministers stalwarts like G.B. Pant followed by Khurshid Lal, Bhakt Darshan, K.C. Pant and N.D. Tiwari, the region has stayed backward, steeped in poverty and corruption. As if in confirmation of this state of affairs, the Allahabad High Court ordered that the region be allowed reservation of 4 per cent of seats in engineering colleges and 6 per cent in medical colleges of the state.

Rise in literacy and the lack of employment in the hills has resulted in 'remittance economy', where a large number of young men go away to the cities in the plains, work and send money home.[19] The women are left behind to tend to the fields and bring up the children. The only job opportunities available to those not selected in to services are as class three and four employees in government offices. A small number are absorbed as teachers.

People had become totally disillusioned with the political games played over the separate state issue. The idea of a state, autonomous unit or region called Uttarakhand, Gangalaya or Uttaranchal goes back to 1950s when one of the CPI's founder leader, P.C. Joshi, raised this issue. Then, former Tehri Raja Manvendra Shah, MP, pleaded for the creation of Uttarakhand, but was sent away to an ambassadorial post. In the later part of 1970s, Uttarakhand Kranti Dal was formed. Its electoral performance was a mixed one. In the early 1990s, the BJP backed the demand but dumped it on the Centre. The demand was raised by some Congress leaders but their eyes were on party tickets or a berth in the cabinet after elections. Poor political representation was an important cause of growing local resentment.

The implementation of Mandal reservations had worsened the situation and the order to implement the UP Panchayat Act, 1994 had added fuel to the fire. The state government's policy of reserving 27 per cent posts/seats

19. *Hindustan Times*, 9 December 1994.

in appointments in government services and admission to educational institutions for socially and educationally backward castes (SEBCs) had made a large number of people apprehensive that outsiders would be the real beneficiaries for the simple reason that SEBCs constitute only 2 per cent of the population of the region. Uptil now, most of the jobs in the region were cornered by the local people because firstly, there is to some extent the 'sons of the soil' feeling among the educated people of the region. Secondly, most plains people viewed such jobs as 'punishment' postings and avoided them. With 27 per cent jobs reserved, the apprehension was not merely that outsiders would come to take up the jobs in the hills but that these jobs might remain vacant. Deprived of job opportunities, with totally uncertain future, the educated youth of the region had no avenues open to them except to add more numbers to the army of unemployed. Another grievance was related to the government's move to carry out a fresh delimitation of *gram sabhas*. This would increase the size of existing *gram sabhas* while decreasing their numbers, thereby reducing funds for various schemes. Due to decentralised planning approach, *panchayats* have become much more attractive. Moreover, bigger *panchayats* are less efficient in the unfriendly terrain in which they are constituted. The situation was compounded by the provocative statements of the then Chief Minister Mulayam Singh Yadav. The movement grew in its intensity. Finally, in September 2000, came the creation of Uttaranchal.

The analysis of the Uttarakhand movement has spawned a rash of student politicians who saw personal profit in the politics of regional identity. Some of them are financed by national leaders of the region. As office-bearer of the union of a college/university, they get various types of favour from district authorities, develop contacts with Centre and state ministers, receive 'donations' from hoteliers, wine shops and restaurant owners. After passing out, most of them become contractors, where their income depends on the benevolence of their political and bureaucratic contacts. In order to fortify their position, they take to politics as a side profession, enthusiastically waving the flag of regionalism. The real issues confronting the people—developmental work like drinking water supply, a proper network of roads and hospitals—has consistently been ignored. And this, more than anything else, is the cause of the widespread discontent among the people.

The creation of Uttaranchal re-energised the demand for Harit Pradesh and Poorvanchal . The former demand is not based on economic backwardness but the reverse—the region's economic prosperity. It is the outcome of the declining influence of the Jats in the state. It is their perception that with the creation of a new state, they will regain the high position they had lost with the passing away of Charan Singh. Since late 1990s, certain political parties, individuals, lawyers and organisations have continuously been raising the demand. After losing the 1996 Lok Sabha election to the BJP, Ajit Singh has gone in whole hog crusading on the issue. Through the platforms of Kisan Vikas Party (KVP), Bhartiya Kisan Kamgar Party (BKKP), Rashtriya Lok Dal (RLD), Paschimi Uttar Pradesh Rajya Nirman Morcha (PUPRNM), Harit Pradesh Nirman Samiti (HPNS) and other political organisations, leaders have tried to mobilise public opinion in favour of a separate western state. Kokab Hamid, MLA from western UP raised the issue several times in the Legislative Assembly. Proponents of a separate state argue that the main reason for the chronic maladministration and lack of development in UP is its size. For an effective and responsive administration, smaller units are more suitable. The development of western UP is insignificant in comparison to its contribution to the state. It has made great contributions to the defence and security of the country, yet it has been neglected by the government. The location of the state capital at Lucknow and the machinery of justice at Allahabad are very far from the region and visiting these cities costs too much and takes too much time. People of the region are discriminated against in government jobs and the academic institutions of the region are given much less grant-in-aid in comparison to those of eastern and central regions. The politicians of eastern area attempt to keep western politicians out of important positions; and there are cultural differences between the two wings of the state. These grievances were raised on several occasions. Leaders supporting the cause, specially Ajit Singh, have persistently organised public meetings, *padyatras*, press conferences, press statements, *jan andolan*, seminars and brainstorming sessions.

The separate state demand is the culmination of the earlier and less extreme demands for a mini secretariat, agricultural university, a bench of Allahabad High Court. Ajit Singh has attempted to mobilise various groups, such as political parties, students, lawyers, the trading community and chambers of commerce in support of a separate state but did not press the issue when his party shared power with the SP. A section of the BJP supports the idea of dividing the state into four parts. The move is supported by the BSP, Rashtriya Kranti Party and the Janata Dal. The Samajwadi Party is opposed to any such move; Mulayam Singh knows very well that in a smaller unit he is sure to lose political weight. However, the Congress Party is not committed either way on this issue.[20]

The demand for Poorvanchal, a separate eastern state, too is not far behind. Several organisations whose names begin with the word 'Poorvanchal' have cropped up, such as Kranti Parishad, Banao Dal, Rajya Sthapana Samiti Sena and Nirman Sangh. Bhartiya Janata Party MP, Yogi Aditya Nath, was earlier reluctant to support the issue, calling it a political gimmick but has changed his stand and declared his support. BSP supremo Mayawati, too, has shown interest in the issue. The argument is that a separate state is the only way to the speedy development of the region. They feel that UP has become a "dysfunctional and lop-sided leviathan". The political importance that the state has been enjoying since Independence has not, the argument goes, resulted in any economic progress. Its unimaginative leadership, administrative inefficiency and corruption have made it into one of the most poorly managed states. But the movement has not received mass support.

While making a case for smaller states, one can learn some lessons from the experiences of the newly formed states and avoid the pitfalls. Has the new state of Uttarakhand addressed the causes for which the new state was demanded? Has the state gained viability by improving the people's quality of life and bringing administration and justice to their doors? Has institutionalisation taken root in the state? No doubt, administration of smaller units is easier, more accessible to the people and is more accountable and transparent. As justice is dispensed close by, it has minimised exploitation and unnecessary harassment. More political leaders have also been accommodated and social welfare activities are fostered better. But the formation of a state is a serious pioneering task with several new aspects. It needs a lot of investment in infrastructure and inevitably, contentious issues relating to boundaries, location of capital and division of assets crop up and are seldom resolved. Reorganisation of UP into four or five states is neither a practical or sensible option. It can, at best be divided into two or three units. Without wasting much time and energy in controlling the movements, the state government should take the initiative to reorganise UP into three states—Awadh, Brijbhoomi or Harit Pradesh and Bundelkhand (including some adjacent states of MP).

But that would be just the beginning. Simply parceling out new states is hardly going to satisfy the rising expectations of the masses. Caught in the

20. *Economic and Political Weekly*, August 4, 2001.

vortex of electoral politics, the real issues of the people are being consistently ignored. The old habit of the establishment to deal with such movements only when they turn violent has set a wrong precedent. "It encourages and strengthens the extremist fringe in the movement to seize the leadership by highlighting the failure of the moderates." The politics of regional identity is reflective of the weakness of local self government. A strong and affective local self government would certainly mollify the sentiments for autonomy. Hence, much needs to be done even after the formation of new states.

The establishment of a political federation should be given primacy. This can be done by establishing inner-party democracy and ensuring the accountability of the local party functionaries. There is an urgent need for nurturing a culture of cooperation and trust among the people and moderation on the part of government. Only then will the nation be able to defeat the forces of disintegration and hold itself together. The harmony between the society 'below' and the political institutions 'above' must be maintained in order to make the national system as a whole much more cohesive and stronger and above all, much more just and responsive.

16 The Case for Reorganisation

S.C. Tripathi

There are two aspects that come to the fore in any discussion about the characteristics of Uttar Pradesh. One is that the state has no single and strong regional or linguistic character. Following from this, one can deduce the second aspect which is that the regional and linguistic aspirations of the OBC movement, having no real rivals, have been very dominant. In states like Tamil Nadu, Maharashtra, the OBC movement has had a chance to project itself through regional representation as well as on linguistic terms but this did not happen in UP. It was there for a short while in the form of the Hindi movement led by the late Socialist leader Ram Manohar Lohia. Many of the present day OBC leaders including Mulayam Singh Yadav and Kalyan Singh had come to the fore initially as followers of Lohia in the Hindi movement. But that movement was not taken forward, despite the fact that UP took pride in calling itself the Hindi heartland of India. As a result, the OBC masses were left with caste as their only identity. This is one of the reasons why the state parties are caste based.

The areas that make up this state has always had a sub-regional identity. The British first called it the 'United Provinces of Agra and Awadh' and then, although it was a province of Agra, they renamed it the 'North West Province'. It extended from near the borders of Punjab to almost the eastern end of what is today called UP. The capital shifted from Agra to Allahabad and finally in 1921 to Lucknow. So, sub-regional identities have been the lot of eastern UP areas, whether they were called Bundelkhandi or Braj, Awadhi or Bhojpuri. As would be expected, these sub-regions, with their weak identities were soon subsumed by the the larger provincial identity. This larger identity itself got merged in the 'heartland' identity, which came in various forms, such as the Hindu heartland, Indo-Islamic heartland, Buddhist heartland, nationalist heartland, cultural heartland and a combination of these various heartland identities.

There is a sense of pride among the people of UP in the belief that they belong to the 'Indian heartland', which acts as a sop to their resentment over not being given their due share of political power. In this context, even the separation of Uttarakhand was painful because it was an issue of Hindu identity. The question asked was: even if Uttarakhand had different economic, geographical and physical characteristics, how could one separate the Ganga from Gangotri and how could holy places like Varanasi, Allahabad, Kashi, Mathura, Ayodhya and Prayag (all situated in Uttar Pradesh) be separated from Badrinath and Kedarnath in Uttarakhand? This was the link between the people of Uttar Pradesh and Uttarakhand. One could even say that there existed between the people some kind of a symbiotic relationship, which they have wanted to maintain whatever be the differences among them.

But ultimately, it was the difference in the social (read caste) composition of the two regions that caused the break. The then Chief Minister Mulayam Singh Yadav wanted to impose the OBC quota in the hill regions too, ignoring the hugely difference caste composition that prevailed there. Precisely 48 per cent belonged to upper caste Thakur community, about 20-25 per cent were Brahmins, about 20-25 per cent scheduled castes and the OBCs constituted a mere 4-5 per cent. Uttaranchal's demography is slightly different now because it has acquired large plain areas. But before the separation, the OBCs constituted less than 5 per cent of the population. It meant that the imposition of the quota system would bring in a large number of people from places like Etawah or Kanpur in central UP, especially the OBCs, who would hog the government jobs, leaving little or nothing for the rest of the people in Uttaranchal. But for this threat, the movement would not have gathered the necessary momentum because the hill people had, perhaps, over a long period become habituated to a life of neglect and underdevelopment.

But now, the basis for the state re-division demands is different in that it is motivated essentially by a growing feeling that the state has become unmanageable for governance and administration. This could well be a valid premise. For one, there is an undeniable tendency to centralisation. Almost every issue, however local or minor, seems to be sent to Lucknow for decision at the top. This, among other reasons, point to the virtues of smaller political and administrative units for efficient governance, particularly for swift decisions. The issue is not about good or bad or the right or wrong decisions because, in the politically surcharged atmosphere that prevails, one would find it difficult to judge whether the decision was right or wrong. What the people are impatient for is quick decisions, so that they can, if necessary, go up to the highest levels and get the decisions amended.

Secondly, the state is bereft of any leader. There is no leader coming forward in Uttar Pradesh who has a popular following in all regions and among all sections of the society. The politics has become a zero sum game, an adversarial exercise where carrying everyone along is not in consideration. For the last 20 years, this kind of politics has served the interests of the few, leaving the rest behind. Things, it is hoped, will change after some time but for the present, the feeling is that there is no leader or leadership with an overall appeal or capability to protect the overall interests of the state. Almost every one believes leadership, too, is taking sides with one region or another, one section of the people or another.

However, my perception is that given the existing economic and social factors, the case for a new governance-administration unit is basically made out only for eastern UP. In fact, the conditions in Bundelkhand, called the 'state of poverty' is not as bad as those in eastern UP which, going by the social indicators, is in the throes of extreme poverty. The only indicators that are bad for Bundelkhand are the geographic and physical indicators that, as always, point downwards, such as the irrigation percentage and productivity. Traces of feudalism remain, which means that there are large land holdings and the percentage of landless workers is slightly higher. Of course, there has been no industrialisation and hence factory workers are much fewer. But indicators of poverty, literacy and some social indices are much better in Bundelkhand than in eastern UP.

The eastern region presents a case of overall underdevelopment. If Gautam Budh Nagar has a per capita income higher than Delhi and may be three times the average per capita income of UP, it means that it has about 7-8 times the per capita income of Kushinagar, Sravasti and such districts. So the difference between western UP (particularly in regions near Delhi) and the rest of UP is widening. Sections of the western UP population naturally feel that they could do much better if they were not a part of UP. This is true, if one analyses the parameters objectively. Similarly, the thinking in eastern UP is that since smaller states get a greater share of resources, perhaps the sensible thing to do is to bring about a condition in which a western leader is not thrust upon them. However poor they were, the eastern people were happy as long as their leader came from among them. But that is no more the case. In this state, 'the leader' means the Chief Minister—the others are of little importance.

So the feeling is developing in eastern UP too. About Bundelkhand, it must also be pointed out that, administratively or politically today, it has only 7 districts. One would think it is just too small to be a state, even if a few 'Bundelkhandi' districts in Madhya Pradesh are joined to it. It is possible only if the Kanpur Division is also merged with Bundelkhand. As for western UP, it would encompass Agra, Meerut, Bareilly and Moradabad division and the rest of UP will make up the eastern state. It will not be painless. There could be riots over sharing of water and many other difficulties will crop up but given the present political, administrative and economic scenario, an immediate and serious thought needs to be given to the option of state re-division.

11. *Economic & Political Weekly*, July 17-24, 1993, p.1524.

An Overview and Some Projections

Venkitesh Ramakrishnan

The primary basis for the ORF seminar that resulted in the compilation of this volume was four factors that have held sway over the state for nearly two decades. These were social churning in terms of identity politics, a long period of political instability that developed along with and partly as a consequence of the ascent of identity politics, the consistent economic backwardness of the state and the aggravation of regional disparities. Over the last decade and a half, these factors had impacted Uttar Pradesh cumulatively and severally creating a distinct impression that the state is unmanageable, politically and administratively. This context had, from time to time, motivated debates, demands and occasional organised struggles highlighting the need to undertake a geographical, political and administrative restructuring of Uttar Pradesh.

The April-May 2007 elections to the State assembly resulted in the formation of a single party government of the Bahujan Samaj Party (BSP) under the leadership of Mayawati. With this, one of the four dominating factors—that of political instability—changed in a decisive manner. Would this change, by itself, have salutary effect on the three other factors that have dominated the state in recent years and thereby on the larger "unmanageable situation" in Uttar Pradesh? There is little doubt that the election result has infused tremendous hopes about a course-correction among vast masses of the public as well as the political class.

However, an assessment of the origins as well as the history of the factors under study indicates that the correction in one sphere alone may not be enough for a comprehensive modification of the maladies faced by Uttar Pradesh. The assessment underscores that the very creation of Uttar Pradesh during the British Raj through the amalgamation of culturally disparate regions is a factor that has contributed significantly to the state's manifold maladies.

Many single party governments have ruled Uttar Pradesh in the six decades of independent India and it was during these very regimes that the "unmanageable situation" developed, in spurts and starts. In such a context, the idea of reorganisation of Uttar Pradesh is still valid for consideration and debate. More so because such debates on reorganisation have risen and acquired concrete political dimensions in relation to other states such as Maharashtra and Andhra Pradesh.

In his seminal essay "Constructing the Heartland: Uttar Pradesh in India's Body Politic", Professor Gyanesh Kudaisya makes a comparison between historian Donald Anthony Low's description of the political culture of Uttar Pradesh in the early decades of the 20th century with the one that exists in the state in the beginning of the 21st century. Low likened UP's dominant politics of early 20th century to an empty shell, "The Flesh had dried up. The Kernel had gone. Only the husk remained." His reasoning was that UP's political culture, monopolised by a dominant elite that subscribed to an Indo-Islamic culture quite distinct from the mass of people who populated the province, lacked substance and hence would be challenged and destroyed by the political mobilisation of the 1920s. According to Kudaisya, when one considers UP's political structure at the beginning of the 21st century, hundred years later, it is tempting to bring into play the same metaphor of the empty shell.[1]

Kudaisya further argued, "UP as a constituent part of India's body politic, as it has come to exist today, finds itself in a mess". "The state's political life lacks a common focus, and is deeply fragmented along the lines of class, caste, religion, faction and region. Its representative and civic institutions are in disarray. It stands almost at the bottom *vis-à-vis* other states in the Indian Union as far as the indices of human development—literacy, per capita income, infant mortality, and female education—are concerned. It is woefully lacking in basic infrastructure and industrial dynamism. Perhaps what is worse, its self constructed identity as the political heartland of India looks increasingly a hollow claim."[2]

Kudaisya's line of argument in relation to UP's identity as the 'political heartland of India' has been summed up as follows in the introduction of the

1. From Gyanesh Kudaisya's paper "Constructing the Heartland: Uttar Pradesh in India's Body Politic", published in the *Journal of South Asian Studies* in August 2002. A shortened version of the essay was published in *Political Process in Uttar Pradesh*, a compilation edited by Sudha Pai and published by Pearson/Longman in 2007.

2. Ibid.

compilation *Political Process in Uttar Pradesh* by Sudha Pai. "Five different but overlapping 'constructions' of UP have emerged over the last 120 years: the colonial, which established the modern rule of law but which was designed to serve imperial interests; the nationalist, which successfully appropriated the colonial construction, thus seriously eroding British authority and making the province the main site of the freedom movement; the notion of UP as the seat of 'Muslim politics', which, however, slipped from its position of prominence after partition. In the post independence period, UP was projected as the repository of the nation's composite culture, a notion that was used successfully to prevent efforts to break up the 'heartland'...From the late 1980s, the Sangh Parivar has tried to make UP simultaneously the site of a resurgent Hindu society and a vote bank."[3]

These varied constructions, however, Kudaisya argues, "have not provided UP with its own selfhood and individuality—in contrast to the States in south India—which could have put it on the path to development. Rather, UP has paid a heavy price for maintaining its self-constructed identity as the 'political heartland', or the most important state in India, which today is an empty claim. Kudaisya concludes that breaking up the state into smaller cultural regions is urgently required. However, to realise UP's creative possibilities and to reestablish its democratic culture the new state must empower those social Groups that have a greater commitment to fostering a regional identity and to working for social development."[4]

Kudaisya's essay was published in August 2002. Much of what he has observed remains relevant to any discourse on the state of polity and the socio-economic situation in UP but with one significant distinction. The 'disarray' that he perceived in the 'representative' institution of the state has given way, through the Assembly elections in April-May 2007, to a potentially stable dispensation.

Changing the History of Rustled Up Coalitions

The April-May 2007 elections to the UP Assembly resulted in a massive victory for the Mayawati-led BSP and the formation of the first single party government in the state since 1991. The perception about the 'disarray' in

3. Pai, Sudha (2007). "Introduction" in *Political Process in Uttar Pradesh*. Pearson/Longman.

4. Kudaisya, Gyanesh (2002). "Constructing the Heartland: Uttar Pradesh in India's Body Politic", in *Journal of South Asian Studies*. August.

'representative and civic institutions' of UP was essentially linked to the history of political instability that characterised the state for nearly 15 years since 1993. All the governments that came to power between 1993 and 2007 were coalition governments rustled up on post-poll alliances between parties that normally functioned at various levels of political and ideological disparities, engineering of defections of Members of Legislative Assembly (MLAs) and political horse-trading. As many as 10 governments had assumed office during this period, including one in 1998, led by Congress leader Jagdambika Pal that lasted barely for 24 hours. The period also witnessed two stints of President's rule with a cumulative tenure of over two years.

The BSP's momentous triumph in the 2007 polls was mainly on account of two factors. First, the consolidation of a large majority of the anti-incumbency vote against the Mulayam Singh Yadav-led Samajwadi Party (SP) government (that was in power for approximately three years, leading up to the election) in its favour, literally making it the rallying point of the anti-incumbency feeling. Second, a new social coalition that the BSP made possible by advancing the political plank of Dalit-Brahmin *bhaichara*. The party had built up this plank painstakingly, over a period of two and a half years (following the Lok Sabha elections of April-May 2004) paying attention to minute political and organisational factors at the grassroots.[5] The Dalit-Brahmin social coalition presented a formidable presence in the electoral arena and this helped the BSP attract large segments of anti-incumbency vote from the minority Muslim community as well as from various other backward castes (OBC) and most backward castes (MBCs). In the process, there was a major depletion from the electoral base of the two national parties, the Indian National Congress and the Bharatiya Janata Party (BJP).[6]

Scholar Sudha Pai placed this aggregation of socio-political support bases as the most concrete manifestation of the effort of parties pursuing 'politics of identity' to construct broad, aggregative, social rainbow identities and build new alignments based on them. Pai pointed out that since its formation in 1984, the BSP has constantly reinvented its identity and changed its strategies of electoral mobilisation *vis-à-vis* other political parties, moving from an almost puritanical and hostile approach characteristic of a narrow identity based movement-cum-party to a more moderate and electorally-oriented political party in response with the changing political situation in remaining

5. Ramakrishnan, Venkitesh (2007). *Frontline*, 4 May.
6. Ramakrishnan, Venkitesh (2007). *Frontline*, 1 June.

within the larger framework defined by Dalit identity and the ideology of Ambedkarism.[7]

She was of the view that the BSP has succeeded, at least in terms of the 2007 Assembly polls, in building a broad social base similar to the former upper caste Dalit-Muslim combination of the Congress, which had helped the party establish single party governments till 1989. The major change, however, was that the BSP-led governance would have a Dalit core. "Historically UP has been governed by social alliances led by the upper caste and classes; the Congress up to the late 1980s and the BJP in the 1990s. The fundamental difference is that in the new social alliance Dalit will occupy a predominant position in the governance structures."[8]

BSP's electoral victory leading to the formation of a single party government, the emergence of the Dalit-Brahmin social coalition under the party's leadership and the consolidation of a number of OBC and MBC communities behind it have been evaluated, by a number of socio-political activists and observers, as a positive development, which could potentially have a far-reaching impact on UP's polity and even impart 'a new focus to its political life'. Chief Minister Mayawati herself has repeatedly stated that the mandate of the 2007 polls is to advance "Sarva Samaj (the entire society) oriented development"[9] and that "there would be no promotion of sectarian Political and developmental ideas".

Satish Chandra Mishra, the Brahmin face of the BSP considered second only to Mayawati in the party, iterated that, "the formation of the single party government as well as the advancement of the accommodative Sarva Samaj concept would practically eradicate the caste-communal tensions and tussles that have dominated the socio-political climate of UP for nearly a decade and a half." This, he held, would consequently lead to the alleviation of the socio-economic backwardness and establishment of a new "Uttam Pradesh" (ideal State) identity to UP.[10]

7. Sudha Pai pointed out that the BSP was clearly pursuing an agenda different from other mainstream parties, both in political content as well as character and this was an important factor in the manner in which it made alliances and broke them. The unqualified transferability of the Dalit vote to nay individual/party was another important factor. This attracted mainstream parties like the Congress and BJP to BSP.

8. Pai, Sudha (2007). "Introduction" in *Political Process in Uttar Pradesh*, Pearson/Longman.

9. Ramakrishnan, Venkitesh (2007). *Frontline*, 1 June.

10. Mishra held the rather simplistic view that if the BSP and 'Behenji' (Mayawati) could take all the castes and communities together during the polls, the government can take all together at the time of governance too and that this would automatically lead to solution of socio-economic problems of the state.

The attempt of the early initiatives of BSP's leadership in governance including the constitution of the ministry is clearly to emphasise the accommodative agenda that seeks to directly address various caste and community groups of the state. In keeping with this, the Mayawati-led cabinet has eight Dalit ministers, five Brahmins, four belonging to the other backward caste (OBC) communities and one each Muslim, Baniya, Thakur and Bhumihar. Among Ministers of State with independent charge there are eleven Dalits, seven OBCs and four each Brahmins, Thakurs and Muslims. The ministry formation exercise came as a great relief to many Brahmin legislators, who had apprehended that Mayawati would form an utterly Dalit-centric, sectarian ministry, given the fact that the party had a clear majority.[11]

Indeed, manoeuvers such as these contain a political message but a number of instances at the grassroots following the formation of the ministry, show that the message or the symbolism of these steps are by themselves not enough to strengthen the concept of *sarva samaj* or an accommodative agenda in governance. These instances have underscored the persistence of caste based tensions and tussles in different parts of UP between the upper caste communities and Dalits. Within a month of the government's assumption of office, the field study for this chapter listed the killing of seven Dalits in the western Uttar Pradesh district of Muzaffarnagar. The study also listed, in the same district, three rape cases where Dalit women were victims.[12] Reports from other areas spread across the state such as Rae Bareli, Mohanlalganj, Lakhimpur Kheri and Mahoba have all emphasised that atrocities against Dalit communities are continuing in spite of the political gains made by the BSP through Dalit-Brahmin *bhaichara*.[13] The field study also revealed that in scores of villages in the districts of Baghpat, Muzaffarnagar and Meerut, Dalits are unable to occupy the *patta* land allotted to them by the government on account of the domination of upper castes on the ground. Repeated orders by the official machinery, from the Chief Minister's office to the district magistrates, have not made an impact in a number of cases. In this context, there have been allegations that many upper caste officers implementing government orders in the lower levels are in collusion with those that have occupied land illegally. In this context, there have been demands by Dalits in

11. Ramakrishnan, Venkitesh (2007). *Frontline*, 1 June.

12. Reports gathered from local police stations in the concerned districts during field study undertaken in July 2007.

13. *Liberation Magazine*, July 2007.

all three western districts to allot fresh *pattas*, designating land that can be actually occupied.[14]

Clearly, the BSP's political success and the movement that paved the way for it have not resulted in the evolution of a new, pervasive social harmony or even awareness about removing caste discrimination. A widely reported case in Mahoba district underlines this aspect. This case highlighted how a Brahmin lady (Urabrani Devi, belonging to Daharra village in Mahoba district) was socially ostracised by fellow Brahmins for the "crime of inviting a few Dalits to a feast held in her house."[15] There have also been reports of arguments and clashes between students owing political allegiance to the BSP and authorities in several educational institutions over the issue of putting up portraits of Dr. Babasaheb Ambedkar in these institutions. In many parts of western Uttar Pradesh, these clashes have disrupted normal functioning of several educational institutions.[16]

In the background of all this, the BSP government in the first year of its governance provide no clarity as to which of the contradictory tendencies—the accommodative *versus* the combative—would ultimately prevail over the political culture of UP and become its dominant political culture. Interpretations of these divergent tendencies have also been multifaceted. Sections of the bureaucracy in the state capital as well as in the districts have been quick to explain away the incidents as a direct result of the "greater sense of power" that Dalits have obtained under the BSP regime. The argument is that such oppressive incidents were happening earlier too but the Dalit society could not be bold then to report it to law enforcement agencies, and now under a 'favourable regime' they are getting around to putting it on record in larger numbers.[17]

On the other side, many interpretations, especially by socio-political observers, have emphasised that the Dalit-Brahmin *bhaichara* and *sarva*

14. Field study in several villages of Meerut district unraveled this plight of Dalits, who have been awarded *patta*. Scores of Dalits were bold to express their demand for alternate *pattas* to this writer. A number of officials also admitted that there was resistance even at the level of *tehsil* officials (officials at lower levels of government).

15. Verma, Amita (2007). *Asian Age*, 7-8 June.

16. Clashes have been reported in the districts of Meerut, Muzzaffarnagar and Ghaziabad right from the end of May 2007 and continued sporadically in June. This writer met many students involved in the "Place Ambedkar photo" campaign during the field study. A group of students in Meerut told this writer that their demand was simple; Ambedkar needs to be placed on the same pedestal as Mahatma Gandhi and Jawaharlal Nehru.

17. A number of bureaucrats including Shailesh Krishna, Principal Secretary to Chief Minister Mayawati expressed this opinion during the field study conducted in July 2007.

samaj concepts are essentially cosmetic and are incapable of bringing about far-reaching changes in polity or society. The view has it that the slogan of "Sarvajan Hitaya" (welfare for everybody) is only a continuation of the "Vasudaiva Kutumbakam" (the world is one family) slogan that has been mouthed by Hindu religious leaders for many centuries. That slogan did not help improve the socio-economic-cultural plight of the oppressed castes and the *sarva samaj* slogan too would, at the moment, only help advance the socio-economic agenda of the higher castes.[18]

The contra-view has highlighted even the Daharra incident as an "intrinsically positive development" stressing that a Brahmin lady made bold, perhaps for the first time, to invite a whole group of Dalits for a feast in an upper caste household in a Brahmin-dominated village.[19] The latter view has been buttressed by stressing that the 2007 elections have marked a sea-change in the attitude of the upper caste Brahmin community, because they have, one way or the other accepted the leadership of a Dalit leader. Whatever the direction the political culture of UP ultimately adopts there can be little doubt that these contradictory tendencies, in essence, reflect and underscore the dynamics of the very political process of the state over the past decade and a half.

The Rise and Growth of Identity Politics

Until the late 1980s there was a kind of predictability about the elections in UP and consequently about the political processes inherent in them. It could be termed in one phrase as "the dominance of the Indian National Congress". The state had 15 Chief Ministers from the time of Independence in 1947 to 1989 and 11 of them belonged to the Congress Party. A number of studies, including by scholars like Paul Brass, have observed that at the time of Independence, the dominant single party system of the Congress was well established in a number of states but the classic example of the system was indeed UP. The party had developed its support base by moulding itself as an 'aggregative umbrella party that had support of almost all sections of the electorate'. "The leadership was of course from the upper castes but it had far reaching support among the lower castes as well as the minorities. In terms of structure the organisation reached down to the village level. It developed and relied on

18. Opinion expressed by Ramesh Dixit, UP State President of Nationalist Congress Party (NCP) during interactions as part of the field study.

19. Opinion expressed by Advocate Indra Bhushan Singh, senior lawyer, Allahabad High Court and political analyst.

an efficient system of vote banks based on the support of local notables. It also developed strong national and regional leadership which ensured over all discipline despite factional tendencies."[20]

The single most important thrust of political processes in the state since 1989 has been that of knocking down of this Congress dominance. And the central factor that has caused this 'knocking down effect' is the politics of identity assertion and political mobilisation along the lines of social cleavages advanced by various political parties. It had developed in three streams in UP, broadly represented by the BJP, BSP and SP, and all three streams had built themselves up on different sectarian socio-political perspectives. The BJP advanced the assertion of a communal identity through the practice of Hindutva politics, while the SP focused on the expansion of a 'backward caste identity' through the assertion of OBC communities, particularly of the numerically significant Yadav community. The BSP's thrust was on Dalit assertion, which had concrete manifestations in terms of social, cultural, economic and political empowerment of the weaker sections of society.

All three streams questioned and challenged, although employing diverse socio-political strategies, tactics and manoeuvers, the supremacy of the higher castes in the political process. While the top leadership of both the SP and the BSP were from OBC and Dalit communities respectively and appealed to their core political base rather directly, the BJP promoted a sort of social engineering in its organisational hierarchy by giving due importance to leaders belonging to upper castes as well as OBCs.[21] The BJP's central political plank of Hindutva visualised the building up of a pan-Hindu political constituency through the aggressive pursuit of a fundamentalist religious ideology. The most concrete manifestation of this, through the late 1980s and the early 1990s, was the politicisation of the dispute over Babri Masjid-Ram Mandir in Ayodhya. This had the volatile impact of creating communal conflict and violence across the length and breadth of UP, as also in other parts of the country.

The first decisive blow at Congress dominance was struck in the 1989 elections to the Lok Sabha and the State Assembly through a combination of

20. From the essay "Uttar Pradesh" published in *State of Politics in India*, published by Princeton University Press, 1968.

21. The promotion of a number of leaders belonging to other backward caste (OBC) communities such as former Chief Ministers Kalyan Singh in UP and Uma Bharati in Madhya Pradesh (during the late 1980s and through the 1990s) was part of this strategy. K.N. Govindacharya, Hindutva ideologue of the 1990s articulated the concept of social engineering within various Sangh Parivar/BJP forums during this period.

the BJP and the Janata Dal, to which the leaders as well as the rank and file currently in the SP belonged. In terms of identity politics this combination brought together the stream of OBC assertive politics represented by the Janata Dal and the pan-Hindu identity politics of the BJP. But this combination was short-lived, obviously on account of the incongruities in terms of ideological and political understanding and practice.

It was the BJP-led stream of promotion of aggressive communal identity that gained ascendancy in the early 1990s. Promoting OBC leader Kalyan Singh as its Chief Minister it captured power on its own in 1991 with 31.45 per cent of the popular vote. This victory had risen visions that the approximately five decade long Congress dominance of the political space of UP would be replaced by a Hindutva-oriented BJP dominance. There were "attempts by protagonists of Hindutva to consecrate UP as the battleground for Hindi, Hindu, and Hindustan."[22] The Hindutva-oriented Sangh Parivar led by the Rashtriya Swayamsevak Sangh (RSS) also believed that UP could be developed as the cultural nerve centre of its ideology because the three major 'divine' sites—Ayodhya, Mathura and Kashi—that it identifies as "places of worship confiscated by Muslim (Mughal) invaders falls in UP."[23]

But this conviction and the efforts that ensued from it faced an anticlimactic outcome in the 1993 Assembly elections (the elections held after the demolition of Babri Masjid, an action that was rated within, as the epitome 'Hindu *gaurav*' or Hindu pride) when the SP and BSP joined together to prevent the BJP's return to power. The 1993 verdict marked the ascendancy of the politics of OBC and Dalit identity assertion over efforts to develop a communal pan-Hindu identity. The SP-BSP coalition, just as the BJP-Janata Dal combination, spilt in less than two years, this time highlighting the divergence between the ideology and practice of OBC assertive politics and Dalit assertive politics.

The overall impact of the rise and growth of identity politics in UP as well as the conflicts engendered by them was indeed complex. In spite of the sectarian content of the ideologies of the three streams as well as the violent manifestations it had almost perpetually, they did 'accelerate' "the process of democratisation creating greater consciousness of caste and communal

22. Kudaisya, Gyanesh (2002). "Constructing the Heartland: Uttar Pradesh in India's Body Politic", *Journal of South Asian Studies*. August.

23. Ibid.

identities accompanied by increased politicisation."[24] The ideologues of the SP and the BSP were not at all defensive when they argued that the emergence of a fragmented multiparty system, the consequent political instability and short-lived coalition governments were all not exactly negative for the creative progression of democracy and democratic values.[25]

Scholar Sudha Pai specifically sums up this trend as follows: "While caste based mobilisation created social antagonism it also challenged upper caste dominance and played a positive role by contributing to the social deepening of democracy. These changes ushered in two developments that fed each other; first the rise of primordial identities in the political arena made the single party system no longer tenable. The second, the decline and the deinstitutionalisation of the latter in turn created room for the mobilisation of narrower sectarian parties thus creating conflict, violence and political instability."[26]

The period since 1993 has been marked by the efforts of the three streams of identity politics to acquire decisive control over the political space of UP. In the process, the political representatives of all the three streams displayed the realisation that a sectarian advancement of the agenda of their core constituency alone would not help them achieve their goal. This in turn led to ideological dilution of their political-organisational praxis too. Thus, the BJP, which had taken its communal, Hindutva-oriented political and organisational initiatives to their peak through the 1989 Shilanyas for the Ayodhya Ram Mandir and the ultimate demolition of the Babri Masjid in 1992, was seen trying to build some understanding with sections of the minority Muslim community in the 2004 Lok Sabha polls. This did generate problems within the Hindutva-oriented Sangh Parivar with leaders of the extremist Vishwa Hindu Parishad (VHP) openly chastising leaders of the BJP for giving upon Hindutva.[27]

Similarly, the SP actively wooed sections of upper caste Thakur community, even while trying to retain its predominantly Yadav core OBC support base and the BSP launched initiatives to win over the Brahmin

---

24. Pai, Sudha (2007). "Introduction" in *Political Process in Uttar Pradesh*. Pearson/Longman.

25. Ramakrishnan, Venkitesh (1999). *Frontline*, 8 October. Apart from the cited article, Kanshi Ram, the founder of BSP had, in several interactions with this writer in the 1980s and 1990s advanced the idea that political instability, in the medium term, was good for the social and political mobility of Dalits. He had maintained that the BSP's strategy of choosing one party and then another as its partner is part of this strategy.

26. See Footnote 24.

27. Ramseshan, Radhika (2002). *The Telegraph*, 25 October.

community. Again, in ideological terms it was perceived that the compulsions of realpolitik has shifted the priorities of this overtly "Socialist" party from egalitarian and peasant-oriented perspective to a moderated pro-liberalisation perspective. The BSP, which, in early years, had aggressively pursued an anti-upper caste, anti-Brahmin line through its famous "Tilak, Tarazu Aur Talwar, Inko Maro Joote Char" (Beat the Brahmins, Thakurs and Banias with slippers) slogan and concept Dalit "Bahujan" advancement moved away to the politics of *sarva samaj* welfare and the concept building alliances between upper castes and Dalits.

This phenomenon has been analysed as follows: "By the second half of the 1990s caste and community based mobilisation had reached a high point and then began to decline. UP politics entered a phase of moderation as the ideology of Hindutva experienced exhaustion and caste based mobilisation reached a plateau. Today parties are attempting to widen their social bases and build broad social alignments because of the compulsions of the electoral politics. BJP is attempting to retrieve lost ground; SP and BSP are engaged in a confrontation as they employ new strategies to build broad aggregative parties in order to capture power."[28] Consequently, the ardent advocacy of political instability as a political device, which would enhance the democratic process, as well as the single-minded pursuit of narrow sectarian agendas based on caste and communal identity have become increasingly moderated.

The central political and organisational message from the 2007 polls is that it is the BSP that has emerged victorious in the political manoeuver aimed at creating an aggregative, core caste-constituency that holds together a wider support base. But the results also show that a major part of this gain was made by chipping away from fellow opposition parties like the Congress and the BJP and not by depleting the BSP's main opponent, the SP. It has been observed that both the BSP and the SP have been at this "political chipping game" since 1998. Both parties had advanced a formula that sought to accentuate its core caste support with permutations and combinations from other castes aimed at enhancing their vote share winning chances. It is this process that has finally led to the consolidation of the Dalit-Brahmin social coalition and the resultant election victory achieved by the BSP in the 2007 polls.[29]

Clearly, this whole process spread over nearly a decade and a half is exceptionally educative for all students of politics and sociology. "The inter play

28. See Footnote 24.

29. Ramakrishnan, Venkitesh (2007) *Frontline,* 1 June.

between identity assertion, mobilization by political parties and electoral politics in UP since the 1980s has transformed the political process in the state."[30] A study of this phenomenon is important for an "understanding of the new post-Congress/post-economic reforms polity that is emerging and its significance for Indian democracy. The process in UP provides an important site for such a study because this is where the identity politics of Hindutva, Mandal, and Dalit—all of which have acquired national importance—are centred."[31]

As is evident from the above narration, the identity based political process of the last decade and a half has been a dynamic one. Its own track record would restrain any observer from making predictions about a lasting phase of stability, in spite of the comfortable majority that the BSP has in the Assembly at present. The social tensions between Dalits and upper castes that have come to the fore following the results is an added factor that strengthens this sense of restraint. The Dalit movement in UP has been built up over the last three decades in a three tier format consisting of the political face in the BSP, a government employees organisation that tracks Dalit welfare programmes of the government in BAMCEF and agitational Ambedkarite grass roots organisations like Dalit Panthers militantly working at the grassroots towards eradication of social discrimination and for Dalit upliftment. Several activists of Dalit Panthers made it clear during the course of the field study for this chapter that whatever the projections and pronouncements of the government, they would continue with their militant advocacy of Dalit causes.[32] The field study for the chapter has also revealed individual reactions from upper caste supporters of the BSP expressing their apprehensions regarding an "extreme, aggressive pursuit of the Dalit agenda" by the Mayawati-led dispensation and their own resolve to "oppose it with all their might".[33]

The other perceived possibility, in terms of political mobilisation, is that of a consolidation of all OBCs and large sections of upper caste Thakur community, behind the SP, in the background of the fact the Congress and BJP are steadily losing their strength to fight a major electoral battle or make their presence felt in the political arena. This supposition is based on the premise that the BSP would retain the Dalit-Brahmin social coalition intact.[34]

30. See Footnote 24.

31. Ibid.

32. Views expressed during interaction for this chapter with Dalit Panther activists of Meerut.

33. Views expressed by Brahmin activists of the BSP including Members of Legislative Assembly.

34. Opinion expressed by Advocate Indra Bhushan Singh, senior lawyer, Allahabad High Court and political analyst.

Obviously, none of these has emerged as concrete or fully blown problems for the BSP government in the early days of its existence. Given the dynamic nature of political maneuverings and mobilisation in the pursuit of identity politics, it is also virtually impossible to pinpoint which of these projections would concretise and if so in what time frame. In the first decade of the 1990s itself there were three trends that alternatively held sway over the political processes in the state, especially in terms of electoral politics. Between 1990 and 1992, the dominant political culture had inclined towards pan-Hindu socio-political-cultural expressions, and between 1993-94 a coalition of Dalits and OBCs emerged as the dominant force and after 1995 all three—politics of Hindutva as well as Dalit and OBC assertive politics—vied for the dominant space. The BSP has certainly assumed that position but given the track record of UP it can be surmised that balancing the hopes and aspirations of BSP's own core constituency of Dalits with that of the new emerging *sarva samaj* support base would not be an easy task for the government.

Questions of Economy and Development

Starting in the late 1980s and through the 1990s, the period during which the 'politics of identity' rose and grew in proportion, UP experienced a steep 'deterioration in its economic growth rate and fiscal health, leading to a severe financial crisis. It represents the backward states within the Union that have performed badly during the period of economic reforms. Placed among the BIMARU states, UP has fallen behind Rajasthan and Madhya Pradesh, which have shown considerable improvement over the last decade. In the ranking of the major states in the Human Development Report 2001, Rajasthan moved from the twelfth to the ninth position, and Madhya Pradesh moved from the fourteenth to the twelfth position but UP dropped from the twelfth to the thirteenth position, slipping to the fourteenth in 1991.

A number of analysts have drawn a direct connection between the rise and growth of the 'politics of identity' and the deterioration of the economic situation. In his essay "Economy of Uttar Pradesh since the 1990s" Ajit Kumar Singh points out that the reasons for the financial deterioration and economic stagnation can be traced to short-lived coalition governments that have followed populist policies to gain the support of various social groups. Competitive populism pursued by political parties has weakened the capacity of the state to undertake developmental tasks and govern effectively. In order to gain electoral support, parties made populist promises to disadvantaged social groups which demanded a share in the fruits of economic development and political power resulting in fiscal crisis. Sudha Pai points to the same factors as follows: "Because of increasing polarisation of electorate no party was able to gain a majority leading to hung assemblies and short lived coalition governments which were unable to formulate effective and long term policies to implement unpopular decisions."

Government records reveal that, in 2006-07, budgetary expenditure on vital areas such as agriculture and allied activities is only 2.41 per cent and on rural development about 3.48 per cent. In contrast, expenditure on administrative services and police was almost 10 per cent of the state's expenditure. The Salary and Pension Bill in 2006-07 amounted to Rs. 23,122 crores leaving very little for developmental programmes. The net irrigated area, electricity generation and food grain production over the last decade has gone down.

Ajit Kumar Singh pointed out that among the major factors responsible for deceleration of growth rates in UP are the declining public investments due to the creeping fiscal crisis and the inability to attract investment from outside due to the poor state of infrastructure particularly power shortage. He was certain that there is a need for a thorough restructuring of the entire system and a sharp break from past policies, practices and priorities.

Ajit Kumar Singh further points out that growth rate in state domestic product (SDP) in UP had remained extremely sluggish during the first four Five Year Plan periods. It started picking up since the Fifth Plan period and caught up with the national growth rate in the Sixth and the Seventh Plan period, with over 5 per cent per annum. However, since the beginning of the 90s growth rate in UP dropped significantly. The sharp deceleration in growth rate of SDP observed since the beginning of the 90s has affected all the sectors of the state economy. GSDP in UP increased at the rate of around 4 per cent per annum during the period from 1993-94 to 2004-05. Trend growth during the period was only 2.0 per cent per annum in case of primary sector (agriculture, animal husbandry, forestry, fishing and mining), and around 4.4 per cent in case of the secondary sector (manufacturing, construction and electricity, gas and water supply) and 4.7 per cent in case of the tertiary sector (transport, warehousing and communications, trade, hotels, banking, insurance, ownership of property, public administration and other social and domestic services).

In the context of the economic deterioration of the past decade, there is a view in sections of the Congress that the parties advancing the 'politics of identity' have an 'intrinsic inability' to adapt to broad based economic vision and carry them forward on account of the very sectarian nature of their political ideology and practice. Advocates of this view point out that the Congress leadership at the time of Independence, led by the 'social thinker' Nehru was able to make itself over, rather smoothly from being a mass, agitationist movement before Independence to being a ruling party that advanced a more or less neatly defined socio-economic vision. This was possible because it had properly assimilated into its political and organisational structure, the various social forces that formed its rainbow coalition support base, had vast organisational following and its thematic thrust was on the concepts of democracy, mixed economy, secularism and federalism. The vision was moderate, centrist and inclusive.

Social and political analyst Hariraj Singh Tyagi finds some merit in this line of thinking and points out that in the initial stages of their growth all the parties of identity had pursued their sectarian agenda aggressively and the very nature of this political practice militated against political adaptability and expediency. "The rise of these 'sectarian' parties in stature and influence at the expense of one party dominance of the Congress, naturally led to the break-down of Congress' economic and development vision." Tyagi holds that the BJP played the biggest role in this process and was responsible for breaking down the Nehruvian consensus on secularism and socialism by advancing what it termed as a Hindu nationalist agenda.

In Tyagi's view, 'intrinsic' adaptation 'inability' that the parties representing 'politics of identity' had was compounded by the fact that a process of economic liberalisation had also been initiated at the national level.

"The core ideology of the liberalisation process involved unleashing of the market forces and this was not in consonance with the Nehruvian 'planned economy' model, which had a significant Socialist orientation. With the onset of economic reforms, development has come to be associated with investment of scarce resources in productive sectors for rapid growth, while welfare is viewed as providing 'support' to the poor and disadvantaged groups. The BJP, which also got to capture power at the Centre during the late 1990s and early 2000s, was particularly confounded by the incongruities between the national compulsion of pursuing liberalisation policies, the heritage of Nehruvian economic model and its own sectarian socio-economic vision on the other. The net result was the pursuit of a half-baked economic policy."

But Tyagi also makes the important distinction that the 'sectarian agenda' and the resultant 'intrinsic' adaptation 'inability' of the parties of identity was only one of the factors for economic deterioration of UP. "One has to take into account the fact that UP has, over the last six decades, typified the slow growth of the country, whether it was under single party dominance or under coalition regimes. Hence, any assessment of UP's backwardness needs to take into account a variety of factors including deficiencies in the economic policies pursued from time to time by different governments, lack of attention to regional specifications such as variations in terms of physical features, human resources and even cultural propensities."

Tyagi's contention needs to be viewed in conjunction with the opinion of many scholars including Pravin Jha and Subrat Das, who have argued that the roots of the fiscal crisis lie in the neo-liberal policies pursued by the Centre. They have pointed out that "from 1986-87 there has been a gradual rise in the fiscal deficit of all states which has increased sharply since 1991-92. Due to a fall in central revenues assistance to the states has declined leaving them with fewer Resources to invest in areas such as infrastructure. In fact the Centre has passed on much of its fiscal crunch to the states. The unleashing of the Market Forces have increased the uneven flow of both assistance and investments thus favouring the better off states at the expense of the poorer states. Thus, the reasons for the deteriorating conditions of State finances are not State specific and lie outside their purview."

The various governments that had occupied power in the 1990s and between 2000-2006 had from time to time addressed the issues of economic deterioration and fiscal deficit. The 'White paper on the Fiscal Situation' issued in 1998-99 was a significant initiative that set in motion a number of measures aimed at course correction. The White Paper identified three major reasons for the fiscal crisis: one, higher growth in revenue expenditure in relation to the growth in revenue receipts; two, declining expenditure on capital formation and low returns on past investments; three, continuous increase in the indebtedness of the state. The World Bank too came out with a study titled "Uttar Pradesh: From Fiscal Crisis to Renewed Growth." A loan was obtained from World Bank in 2001 for fiscal management. This led the UP government to prepare a blueprint of wide ranging economic reforms, covering fiscal reforms and fiscal administration, restructuring public enterprises, power reforms and governance and civil reforms. Based on these reforms UP became the first recipient at the sub-national level of fiscal restructuring from the World Bank.

Following this, the government presented a Medium Term Fiscal Reform Policy along with its budget in 2000-01 and in 2004, the Mulayam Singh Yadav-led SP Government passed the Fiscal Responsibility and Budget Management Act which put forward the principles of fiscal management disallowing the state to spend beyond a certain limit. All this did lead to some improvement in fiscal indicators, especially during 2005-06 and 2006-07. As a consequence there was greater allocation of funds for priority areas like power, roads and health.

This track record of the last two decades and its various dimensions must lay heavily on the Mayawati-led BSP Government as it tries to advance its concept of *sarva damaj* welfare "in order to turn UP into what it terms as Uttam Pradesh." Balancing the contradictions between the economics of liberalisation and the politics of empowerment and evolving a 'middle path' would be one of the major challenges in this regard. Mayawati has had three earlier terms as Chief Minister, heading short-lived coalition governments with the BJP. The primary thrust in each stint was sectarian and sought to promote and nurture the interests of the BSP's core Dalit support base. Mayawati has gone on record that in her earlier stints she was constrained by the limitations of being in a coalition government but this time she would able to work without those constraints in the interests of *sarva samaj* because the BSP has got a majority on its own in the 2007 elections.

Conclusion

The verdict of the 2007 Assembly polls has been perceived as the culmination of a period of tumult that lasted for nearly a decade and a half. The period had presented picture of a complex State with major upheavals in society, polity and economy, leading to sustained political instability, societal tensions and economic deterioration. Given this background, the emergence of the BSP in single party governance and the party's promise to eschew sectarian agendas and evolve a *sarva samaj* government has raised hopes across the state. Yet, it is clear that the government would have to encounter extreme manifestations of the social contradictions that still persist in many forms across the length and breadth of Uttar Pradesh. These contradictions make advancement of a unified political practice and economic development a difficult task, especially in the background of the conflicting pressures of economic liberalisation and the politics of empowerment.

Different economic affairs analysts have highlighted varied and contrasting ideological perspectives on how to address the issue of economic deterioration but the fact remains that the quantum of government in economic development has shrunk over the past decade and a half and is continuing to shrink. The government is ceasing to be the largest employer of people, public investments are declining and the reach of private sector is expanding systematically even in sectors like infrastructure development in crucial areas like power generation, irrigation and agriculture.

The regional disparities in terms of social and economic infrastructure as well as in terms overall development in Uttar Pradesh further complicate the tasks before the government. The government can hope to stabilise the present sense of discord only if it takes special care to overcome the regional disparities without mechanistically adhering to the ideology and political structure of an imagined 'Hindi heartland' in UP. The concept of regional planning is perhaps the only procedure available within the present political and geographical parameters of Uttar Pradesh but past experience *vis-à-vis* the implementation of the concept militates against reposing too much faith in it.

The murmurs within the Manmohan Singh-led United Progressive Alliance (UPA) government at the Centre about setting up a new SRC to look at the possibility of carving out new States based on "a development question" is undoubtedly influenced by UP's experience in the past decade and a half.[35] As Sunil Khilnani has pointed out, the strength of the "idea of India" is that it is "revisable". Uttar Pradesh, its people and their leadership would have to undertake this revision in due course and along with issues of development and economy, the concept of the 'heartland' would also have to come under revision.

35. George, Verghese (2007). *The Indian Express*, 9 July.